UNIVERSITY OF ST. THOMAS LIBRARIES
WITHDRAWN
UST
Libraries

A PUBLIC CHARITY

Polis Center Series on Religion and Urban Culture
David J. Bodenhamer and Arthur E. Farnsley II, editors

A PUBLIC CHARITY

Religion and Social Welfare
in Indianapolis,
1929–2002

MARY L. MAPES

INDIANA UNIVERSITY PRESS
BLOOMINGTON AND INDIANAPOLIS

This book is a publication of

Indiana University Press
601 North Morton Street
Bloomington, IN 47404-3797 USA

http://iupress.indiana.edu

Telephone orders   800-842-6796
Fax orders   812-855-7931
Orders by e-mail   iuporder@indiana.edu

© 2004 by Mary L. Mapes
All rights reserved

No part of this book may be reproduced or utilized in any form or by any means, electronic or mechanical, including photocopying and recording, or by any information storage and retrieval system, without permission in writing from the publisher. The Association of American University Presses' Resolution on Permissions constitutes the only exception to this prohibition.

The paper used in this publication meets the minimum requirements of American National Standard for Information Sciences—Permanence of Paper for Printed Library Materials, ANSI Z39.48-1984.

Manufactured in the United States of America

Library of Congress Cataloging-in-Publication Data

Mapes, Mary L. (Mary Lynne)
A public charity : religion and social welfare in Indianapolis, 1929–2002 / Mary L. Mapes.
p.   cm.—(Polis Center series on religion and urban culture)
Includes bibliographical references and index.
ISBN 0-253-34480-8 (cloth : alk. paper)
1. Social service—Indiana—Indianapolis.   2. Church charities—Indiana—Indianapolis.   3. Public welfare—Indiana—Indianapolis.   4. Nonprofit organizations—Indiana—Indianapolis.
I. Title.   II. Series.
HV99.I5M37   2004
361.7′5′0977252—dc22
2004006414

1   2   3   4   5   09   08   07   06   05   04

For Peter

CONTENTS

ACKNOWLEDGMENTS ... ix
INTRODUCTION ... 1

I   Catholic Charities and the Making of the Welfare State ... 12
II   A City of Families: Social Welfare and Postwar Prosperity ... 32
III   Rediscovering Poverty, Redefining Community: Religion, the Civil Rights Movement, and the War on Poverty ... 61
IV   "Beyond Religious Boundaries": Urban Ministry and Social Order ... 91
V   "One Soul at a Time": Welfare Reform and Faith-Based Organizations ... 119

NOTES ... 149
INDEX ... 169

ACKNOWLEDGMENTS

After completing my Ph.D. in 1998, I was invited to join the Polis Center at Indiana University–Purdue University Indianapolis, where the research and writing of this book occurred. The Polis Center gave me time and access to resources. I am truly grateful. The support of the center's director, David Bodenhamer, was especially important to me as I began my career as a historian. Colleagues Etan Diamond, Art Farnsley, and Elfriede Wedam each contributed significantly to the book. Etan was always willing to listen to my ideas, and he carefully read and edited various chapters. Art challenged me to sharpen my arguments and think more broadly. Elfriede also read most chapters in addition to providing me many warm meals. Other members of the Polis Center who deserve mention include Kevin Armstrong, Vicky Cummings, David Licht, Dawn Parks, and David Vanderstel. Jan Shipps provided especially warm encouragement.

Although this book was begun after I completed graduate school at Michigan State University, the support I received from professors Norman Pollack, David Bailey, and Lisa Fine gave me the skills and confidence to begin this new project. Norman Pollack, my dissertation advisor, always encouraged me to think not about the most recent historical fads but about the meaning of larger, timeless issues, including the meaning and practice of democracy. I hope that this book speaks successfully to those larger issues.

Many institutions made this book possible. I would like to thank the Lilly Endowment, especially Craig Dykstra, for generously funding the Polis Center. The staffs at the Indiana Historical Society, the Indiana State Library, the Catholic Archdiocese of Indianapolis, the United Way, the National Archives in Washington, D.C., and the Catholic University of America helped me identify and gain access to the sources used in the book. The staff at Indiana University Press, most notably Robert Sloan, deserves special thanks for helping this first-time author make her way through the publication process. I would also like to thank Drew Bryan, the copy editor.

The support of family members is especially appreciated. My father, Lynn Mapes, always expressed interest in the book, and my mother, Dorothy Mapes, consistently aided me in good times and bad. The friendships I share with my sisters, Lynne Mapes-Riordan and Christine Mapes-Pearson, were a constant source of support. My nephews and nieces have been a sheer joy, forcing me to enjoy many of the sweeter things in life. Kathleen Mapes, my twin sister, who is also an American historian, has been both a best friend and a supportive critic. Since my first year in college she has read everything I have written, including this book, which she improved considerably with her insightful comments. Finally, I would like to thank my husband, Peter R. D'Agostino, also a fellow historian, who carefully edited the entire book. His patience, love, and support have made the completion of this book possible.

A PUBLIC CHARITY

INTRODUCTION

In 1938, a girl pregnant with her first child arrived at Indianapolis's Suemma Coleman Home for unmarried mothers. When the women running the home learned that the girl was Catholic, they quickly contacted St. Elizabeth's Home, the city's Catholic home for unwed mothers. Although the Suemma Coleman Home was not an official Protestant institution, the city's social workers had long accepted that the Coleman Home would serve Protestant girls, St. Elizabeth's the city's Catholic girls, and the Jewish Family Service Society Indianapolis's Jewish girls. A clear religious division of labor defined maternity home care.[1]

In 1992, when Stephen Goldsmith became mayor of Indianapolis, he initiated a restructuring of city government to privatize public services and encourage "public-private partnerships." He called upon city churches to address social problems. His most visible initiative, the Front Porch Alliance, encouraged clergy and their parishioners to take responsibility for the social ills plaguing neighborhoods. In justifying his outreach to religious institutions, Goldsmith claimed they had previously played an important role in the city and that it was the rise of the "big government systems such as welfare" that had "marginalized" them.[2]

Although Goldsmith's assertion about the historic role of religious organizations in the city's social welfare system was correct, his contention that the welfare state had "marginalized" them was erroneous. The relationship between public and private social welfare agencies has been much more complex. Certainly since the New Deal of the 1930s, government authorities have assumed greater responsibility for social welfare. However, the expansion of public programs did not always result in the withering of private ones. Rather than compete with the private sector, public authorities in Indianapolis—who were fiscally conservative—often turned to private institutions, including religiously affiliated ones, to supplement the services offered by public agencies and in some cases to administer publicly financed programs.

Using the New Deal, the War on Poverty, and the recent turn to faith-based organizations as benchmarks, I explore the relationship between religion and social welfare in Indianapolis within a national context. I evaluate the extent to which Indianapolis participated in or resisted the trajectory of national social welfare trends, highlighting three questions. First, what role have religious organizations played within the city's larger social welfare matrix, both its public and private sectors? Second, how have the more general relations between the public and private sectors evolved? And third, how have notions of citizenship affected the delivery of social services? The answers to these questions reveal that in Indianapolis, religious boundaries helped define social services both when the welfare state expanded its responsibility and when it devolved authority to private citizens.

In the last two decades social welfare historians have discussed in detail the emergence of the welfare state, examining how and why the state emerged as the central actor. Much of this work focuses, rightly so, on the 1930s, when the New Deal's Social Security Act established Aid to Families with Dependent Children, and on the 1960s, when the Great Society introduced such initiatives as Medicare, Medicaid, and the Community Action Program. We now know a great deal about the development of policy at the national level, and we continue to learn more about the delivery of services locally.[3] Studies that focus on gender and race have been especially helpful in deepening our understanding of the values and assumptions that have structured the American welfare state.[4]

Less well understood is what relationship public authorities had with private social welfare organizations. Because public agencies provided considerably more material assistance and grew at a much faster rate than private agencies, it might seem unnecessary to consider the relations between these two sectors. There are, however, a number of historians who argue that public programs should not be examined in isolation from the private sector because historically, the line dividing the two has been far from clear, particularly

Introduction 3

in the late twentieth century. Michael Katz, for instance, insists that an examination of the "blurred boundaries" between public and private social welfare will illuminate the practical and ideological underpinnings of America's "semiwelfare state."[5] Such a focus clarifies how public resources have never been sufficient, and how aid continues to be cast as a charitable endeavor rather than a right of citizenship.

Theda Skocpol suggests that these "blurred boundaries" challenge those who believe that the welfare state has displaced voluntary activity. She shows that voluntary activity and associations have expanded rather than contracted since the state took on a greater role in social welfare. Skocpol points to the post–World War II era, when the American Legion both championed and benefited from the GI Bill, which provided generous social programs to returning soldiers. She concludes: "Far from public social provision and voluntarism being opposed to one another, as today conservatives so loudly claim, they have actually flourished in full symbiosis."[6]

Political scientists and policy studies scholars have provided further insight into these blurred boundaries on the national level. Focusing on the period following 1967—when the U.S. Congress amended the Social Security Act to encourage the states to channel public funds to private social welfare organizations—researchers from these fields have documented the many linkages between the public and nonprofit sectors and discussed in depth the impact that the federal budget cuts of the 1980s had on the nonprofit sector.[7] Although most of this scholarship investigates secular rather than religious nonprofits, it nonetheless reveals the interdependence of government and private agencies.

Two recent events have compelled scholars to consider the role of religious nonprofits in public initiatives. First, in 1996 the U.S. Congress, revamping the nation's social welfare system, abolished the New Deal program Aid to Families with Dependent Children and passed the Personal Responsibility and Work Opportunity Act, which through its Charitable Choice provision allows religious congregations to apply for federal social welfare funding. While religious nonprofits had long had access to public monies, never before had congregations been permitted to receive federal money directly.

Second, in one of his first measures as president, George W. Bush acted on the Charitable Choice provision and announced his faith-based initiative to encourage churches to apply for federal social welfare funds to support a wide range of services from job training to drug rehabilitation.

While legal scholars, in response to these developments, have investigated the constitutional implications for the First Amendment's separation of church and state, political scientists, sociologists, and social workers have set out to explore the capacity and efficacy of faith-based social service.[8] Although focused on current policy, this scholarship raises important questions about the historical roots of faith-based organizations. I discuss those historical roots by focusing on the relationship between religiously affiliated social welfare organizations and public agencies. In the last seventy years, religious social welfare agencies in Indianapolis and other urban centers have provided a wide range of services. In the middle of the century, religious social services provided care for dependent children, unwed mothers, and homeless men. More recently they have tackled such problems as legal representation and housing. Public monies—local as well as federal—have proved critical to their ability to provide such care.

Although religious groups in almost all U.S. cities have contributed to the welfare of urban residents, the degree to which they have participated in social welfare endeavors varies from city to city and state to state. An analysis of one city, this book remains attentive to the way local politics and practices shaped social welfare even as it maintains a concern for the larger national scene. Indianapolis, a mid-sized city whose metropolitan population has risen from less than 500,000 in 1930 to more than 1 million in 2000, is an ideal place to explore the relationship between public and private social welfare.[9] Since the 1930s, public authorities have worked diligently both to minimize expenditures and to keep its "bureaucratic" apparatus small. They achieved these objectives by keeping alive the notion that social welfare was a responsibility of private citizens rather than the body politic and by looking to the private sector to help deliver services.

Home to a conservative tradition, Indianapolis offers an especially valuable vantage point from which to consider the national context. At those times when public responsibility for social needs increased—most notably during the 1930s and 1960s—Indianapolis worked against national trends, or negotiated them uneasily. In rhetoric and practice, Indianapolis more closely resembled neighboring southern rather than northern cities, where most innovations in social welfare practices were created. Social welfare professionals traditionally viewed the state of Indiana as a whole as backward rather than forward-looking. However, in the 1990s and into the twenty-first century, when policy makers are looking to the private sector to solve social ills, Indianapolis has been touted as a model. National figures, including President George W. Bush, have praised Indianapolis for its use of the private sector, and faith-based organizations in particular, in addressing the city's social ills. Indianapolis's relationship to the national story is complex, important because it has both resisted national trends and led them. In either case, Indianapolis provides a barometer for demonstrating how much national policy and ideas have changed.

Indianapolis's religious, political, and cultural heritage has profoundly influenced the city's social welfare system. Long known as the "northernmost southern" city, it has hosted populations with cultural roots in the American North and South. Indianapolis's first settlers in the mid-nineteenth century comprised migrants from Ohio, Kentucky, Pennsylvania, Virginia, and North Carolina, in addition to immigrants from Germany and Ireland.[10] In the late nineteenth and twentieth centuries, migration from the upper South, both black and white, increased dramatically, infusing a southern flavor to the growing northern metropolis. Largely missing from Indianapolis were southern and eastern European immigrants, Catholics, and Jews, who settled in other industrial cities. At the turn of the century, when the foreign-born dominated most urban populations, they constituted less than 10 percent of the population of Indianapolis.[11] Indianapolis took pride in its self-described status as a 100 percent–American town.

These settlement patterns created distinctive religious demographics. According to the 1990 Glenmary statistics, a breakdown of the city's total "church-going" population reveals that Protestants constitute just under 80 percent of the population. Catholics boast the largest denomination, approximately 20 percent of the city's religious residents. (Catholics constitute a much smaller percentage of the total population.) Jews make up a meager 2 percent.[12] Indianapolis has seen the number of evangelical Protestants rise since the 1960s as the mainline's presence has diminished.

Politically, Indianapolis has lived up to its reputation as the northernmost southern city. Until the 1960s, racial and class hierarchies found full expression in civic and political arenas, with segregation in force and wealthier white citizens in control of most important political offices. Furthermore, the city took great pride in its tradition of "Hoosier independence." Although Indianapolis's governing structure has strong ties to the state legislature, city authorities have always prized their ability to make decisions without outside federal interference. Thus while the city participated as early as the 1930s in Social Security programs (including Aid to Families with Dependent Children), it refused until the mid-1960s to participate in other federal programs, most notably federal highway construction. Moreover, the city kept careful count of the amount of federal taxes Indiana residents sent to the federal government and the amount they received back in services. Paradoxically, then, the state on the one hand resisted accepting funds for fear of becoming "dependent" even as it lamented the dollars that "stayed in Washington." Indiana was one of the few states where residents not only preached but also acted on their anti–federal government rhetoric.

The political climate changed dramatically in the mid-1960s, when, under the leadership of Mayor John Barton, a Democrat, Indianapolis fully participated in federal programs, including social welfare. However, this break with the past provoked vigorous debate, and older traditions persisted. Believing that social needs were a private rather than a public responsibility, the city actively encouraged voluntary social agencies to deal with urban social ills, and it referred clients seeking assistance from public authorities to private agencies.

While it was not uncommon for public authorities to help allay the cost that private agencies incurred, authorities remained committed to the idea that private solutions were the best. This political and cultural tradition helps explain why Indianapolis enthusiastically embraced the faith-based initiatives of both Mayor Stephen Goldsmith and President George W. Bush. After decades of resisting or begrudgingly accepting national trends in social welfare, Indianapolis in the 1990s stood at the forefront of current policy. This was not because Indianapolis changed its trajectory and mission, but because the nation adopted a philosophy and specific aims that reflected long-standing traditions and goals in Indianapolis. National politicians have looked to Indianapolis as a model for faith-based work, and Indianapolis natives such as Goldsmith have taken on national stature in public debates. Ironically, then, Indianapolis became a trendsetter not because it adopted a new set of values but because it remained committed to its traditions.

Without narrating a comprehensive history of the city's social welfare system, I elucidate the general trajectory of the city's social welfare policy within a national context by highlighting several exceptionally revealing cases. Beginning with the New Deal, chapter 1 describes how Catholic Charities responded to and affected the shape of the emerging welfare state in Indianapolis. National studies of Catholic Charities, most notably Dorothy M. Brown and Elizabeth McKeown's *The Poor Belong to Us,* have demonstrated how Catholic social agencies significantly influenced the welfare state, shaped national policy, and guaranteed a future for Catholic social programs in both urban and rural locales. In Indianapolis, Catholic Charities recognized that governmental action was necessary, but it still safeguarded a role for Catholic social programs. Like Catholic social agencies elsewhere, Catholic Charities of Indianapolis found new life by harnessing itself to the growing welfare state. With donations falling and volunteer efforts declining, Catholic Charities eagerly accepted federally funded Works Progress Administration (WPA) workers. The county welfare department agreed both to send Catholic children in need of foster care to Catholic Charities and to fund their support. Catholics insisted they had a right to care for "their own" and to do so with tax dollars. They contended that their responsibility to protect the religious "rights" of Catholic children should guarantee them a place in the city's emerging social welfare system. Catholic success in Indianapolis demonstrates how well they learned to negotiate the emerging public welfare system.

For its part, the county welfare department turned to Catholic Charities and other private agencies to preserve its fiscal conservatism and to keep alive the notion that social welfare was a private responsibility. In turning to religious institutions to secure care for the city's needy children, the public welfare department acknowledged that the city had a pre-existing welfare system defined by both religious and racial boundaries. Indeed, city social workers had for decades recognized Catholic, Jewish, and Protestant responsibilities for "their own" and acquiesced to the city's racial divide. Hence, when the public welfare bureaucracy emerged in Indianapolis, it appropriated existing religious and racial boundaries.

The 1940s and 1950s, the focus of chapter 2, are the most understudied decades in American social welfare history. The issue of poverty largely disappeared from the national picture as the national economy boomed and popular culture idealized the middle-class family. Social workers increasingly directed their attention not to the poor but to the middle class. They argued that the origin of social problems was primarily psychological rather than material and that all classes could benefit from their assistance. This was especially true of privately employed social workers, who exercised greater discretion over the clientele they served than social workers employed by public agencies did. In a city where resistance to the New Deal remained high and concern for the poor unpopular, this conservative turn proved attractive. Secular providers, most notably the Family Service Association, accepted without question that the middle class was in need of their services. Although this notion was challenged by evangelical Protestants who rejected the psychological explanations of social ills, Jewish, Catholic, and mainline Protestant social agencies followed the example of the secular providers who drew upon psychological concepts and emphasized that they served all classes, not only the poor. Beginning in the late 1920s, the Jewish Welfare Federation had begun to shift its focus from social welfare to social activities as the class composition of its community changed from largely lower-class to mostly middle-class. In the 1940s and 1950s, Catholics and mainline Protestant agencies maintained their concern for the underprivileged—and in the case of Catholic Charities continued to receive public funds—but they too began to focus greater attention on middle-class families, offering their more prosperous clients marriage counseling, family counseling, visiting homemaking, unwed mother care, and adoption services.

The way in which the nation understood urban social ills changed dramatically in the 1960s with the publication of books like Michael Harrington's *The Other America* and the creation of new federal programs, including the War on Poverty, which is the subject of chapter 3. In 1965, after city authorities broke with tradition and accepted federal money, the War on Poverty arrived in Indianapolis with the creation of Community Action Against Poverty (CAAP), the city's local poverty board. Religious leaders and laity quickly mobilized to use their churches to house CAAP programs and to participate in policy debates. The democratization of politics in the wake of the War on Poverty instigated conflict for control and resources. Conservatives, many of whom opposed the use of federal funds, sought to undermine the War on Poverty. African Americans and their clergy, in contrast, supported the federal initiative as a means to challenge their second-class citizenship.

African American clergy aligned with white liberals battled the Indianapolis political establishment and public welfare authorities to empower poor African Americans during the War on Poverty. Like civil rights activists in cities across the nation, they looked to the federal mandate for "maximum feasible participation" of the poor in the planning and administration of War on Poverty programs. African Americans believed that social welfare policy ought to be a vehicle to challenge racial and class inequalities and to expand the social and civil rights of all urban residents. These clergy brought attention to the interconnections between race and economics as well as the impact of both on evolving notions of citizenship.

Chapter 4 examines the national congregation-based urban ministry movement that began in the 1950s, reached its zenith in the 1960s, and declined precipitously in the 1970s and 1980s. Across the nation, organizations such as Catholic Charities and the Salvation Army had been involved in social services since the nineteenth century. Congregations, however, tended to be places of worship, and prior to the 1960s few contributed significantly to the delivery of social services or programs. This changed in the late 1950s and 1960s as urban congregations responded to white flight and rising poverty rates. In Indianapolis, the ecumenical associations and religious nonprofits that developed from congregation-based urban ministries won federal funds in the late 1960s. In particular, congregations collaborated to establish a housing nonprofit heavily dependent on public funds.

In the late 1990s, religion once again figured into social welfare policy. The Charitable Choice provision of the 1996 Welfare Reform Act and President Bush's faith-based initiative demonstrate how, more than ever before, policy makers at the federal, state, and municipal level are looking to religious congregations to help solve entrenched social ills. Indianapolis has taken a lead in this new national trend, which is the subject of chapter 5. Former Mayor Stephen Goldsmith (1992–2000), best known for his privatization policies, initiated the Front Porch Alliance in 1997 to encourage clergy to play a more active role in their neighborhoods. The Alliance earned Indianapolis a reputation as a national leader for faith-based initiatives. Governor Frank O'Bannon, who believed Indiana's citizens supported new roles for congregations as social service providers, created FaithWorks to help congregations participate in Charitable Choice.

This last chapter focuses on both Indianapolis-based and national faith-based initiatives within the larger context of federal and state welfare reform. In the early 1990s, many states instituted welfare reforms that severely limited the amount of public assistance that the poor could gain access to. When in 1996 the federal government abolished the New Deal program AFDC, it too imposed strict time limits on the poor who received services, while also shifting responsibility to the states, who were free to "contract out" federally funded services to the private sector. The religious sector is the one that policy makers are most eager to collaborate with. Supporters of faith-based organizations argue that religious groups are better suited to deal with social ills because they are ostensibly less bureaucratic, more aware of their neighborhoods, and more in tune with the specific needs of individuals. They claim that the most promising attributes of faith-based organizations are the spiritual and moral values they bring to their work.

In light of the attention Indianapolis has received as a model for faith-based initiatives, its new programs merit close examination. Chapter 5 explains how most churches are neither capable of nor interested in delivering social services, despite the optimistic pronouncements of Goldsmith and Bush. Aggressive efforts to recruit churches—both in Indianapolis and across the nation—have yielded surprisingly few results. So why are advocates of faith-based initiatives so committed to their policies? *A Public Charity* illuminates their resolve by placing current policy goals within a larger political context and a longer historical narrative.

Faith-based initiatives reflect a rightward turn in politics to minimize public responsibility for social ills and devolve government functions to private authorities. The implications of this political shift for the meaning of citizenship and the practice of democracy are immense. By turning to churches, policy makers have revived the nineteenth-century assumption that the moral failures of the poor rather than structural inequalities cause poverty. In addition, they have reinforced the ideologically driven assumption of privatization advocates who argue that government agencies are by definition inefficient and ill-equipped to deal with social problems, and that the private sector—whether the nonprofit or for-profit arm—is always more effective. This conceptualization of the American commonwealth guarantees not only that decisions about the underprivileged are taken out of the public arena and shifted to the private sector, but that assistance for the poor is viewed as a public charity rather than a right of citizenship. As gifts rather than rights, social services can be withdrawn with little fanfare. The nation's failure to include basic social needs within its larger definition of citizenship further marginalizes the most vulnerable from the larger body politic.

I

CATHOLIC CHARITIES AND THE MAKING OF THE WELFARE STATE

In the spring of 1935, Bishop Joseph E. Ritter invited Weltha Kelley, a social work professor from Saint Louis University, to conduct a formal evaluation of the services offered by Catholic Charities of Indianapolis. After interviewing the men and women who worked for Catholic Charities and visiting other private and public social welfare agencies, she concluded, "social work in Indianapolis follows sectarian lines."[1] In an interview three years later, a social worker employed by the newly created public welfare department explained that private agencies continued to play a central role in the city's social welfare system, even after the development of many public programs. Like Ms. Kelley, she found that "division of work on a sectarian basis is thoroughly understood and accepted by the community."[2]

Even though these two social workers emphasized private agencies and their religious character in Indianapolis, we know very little about private social welfare agencies that survived the Great Depression, and even less about their relationship to the emerging welfare state.[3] The history of private social welfare seems trivial alongside the story of the emerging welfare state. But contemporary perceptions of social work in Indianapolis in the 1930s suggest that the whole story of social welfare cannot be told unless we look at public and private agencies and the relationship between them.

* * *

In the 1930s, local social welfare agencies across the nation were granted significant authority over state and federal programs as well as locally funded initiatives. Consequently, communities could imprint their own values onto the programs they administered. For example, public officials in southern states were especially adept at using their power over social welfare programs to reinforce racial hierarchies and regulate labor markets.[4] In northern states, ethnic and racial divisions as well as fiscal concerns affected the distribution of aid.

Local variation was no less significant in the conservative city of Indianapolis. As public bodies gained greater responsibility for social welfare, they worked to keep public expenditures to a minimum and the size of the welfare bureaucracy small. To achieve these objectives, they limited assistance to "worthy" residents. Furthermore, they looked to the private sector to supplement services offered by public agencies and, in some cases, to administer publicly funded programs. As a result, during the 1930s, the ever-shifting boundary separating public and private social welfare became even more blurred in Indianapolis. This chapter examines this shifting boundary by focusing on Catholic Charities of Indianapolis, which, though it was affiliated with a religious minority, successfully claimed new resources from the expanding welfare state.

The intensified overlapping of the public and private sectors in the 1930s proved especially appealing to the men and women working at Catholic Charities. During the Depression they argued that public authorities needed to take greater responsibility for the poor, but nevertheless they wished to maintain a role for Catholics in the city's social welfare system.[5] Having already established their right to care for the city's Catholics, the leaders of Catholic Charities justified their claim to public money in the 1930s by referring to their rights as citizens to protect their own. Even though Catholic Charities could not administer federal funds, it could and did receive state and local money. Rather than finding itself squeezed out by the expanding welfare state, Catholic Charities found new life by harnessing itself to it. As a result, Catholic Charities of Indianapolis, which in 1929 was quite small and not powerful, became by the late 1930s a serious force in the city's social welfare landscape.

Confronting the Great Depression

Known as the crossroads of America, Indianapolis is unique among America's cities. Only a small number of the Catholic and Jewish immigrants who settled in urban America during the late nineteenth and early twentieth centuries chose to make Indianapolis their home. At a time when Catholics and Jews staked out cultural and religious space in so many of the nation's cities, Indianapolis remained predominantly Protestant. By the 1930s, Catholics made up just over 9 percent of the total population and Jews only 2.4 percent.[6] The rest of the population was either affiliated with a Protestant denomination or nominally Protestant. Because the Catholic community was so small, its leaders had had limited economic and political resources to build a social welfare system. Unlike the bishops overseeing Chicago and New York, who in the decade preceding the Depression constructed formidable religious and charitable structures that mirrored Catholic power in public life, the bishop of Indianapolis rarely occupied the city's public stage and built relatively few imposing structures.[7] Furthermore, Indianapolis Catholics in the 1920s were keenly aware that many Protestants, especially those affiliated with the thriving Ku Klux Klan, believed that Catholics could not be fully American.[8]

As a result, when the Depression engulfed Indianapolis, the services offered by Catholic Charities were meager, consisting of a home for unwed mothers, a home for troubled girls, residential facilities for "friendless women" and the aged, and a Catholic Community Center, which provided a low-cost cafeteria and emergency aid. Although these services paled in comparison to Catholic welfare in cities with large Catholic populations, the bishop of Indianapolis had hoped that his people would become more influential when he had led the effort to centralize Catholic social welfare programs under the umbrella of Catholic Charities in 1919. The limitations of Catholic Charities quickly became apparent when the Depression hit the city with full force in the early 1930s. Reflecting the belief that the Catholic poor were the responsibility of the Catholic community, Catholic Charities strove to provide for "all who come to the Center and seek its aid."[9] But because Catholics worked in those industries hit hardest by the Depression, it did not take long before the workers at Catholic Charities recognized that private charity would not suffice and began to seek out other ways to help the poor. They looked first to the Township Trustees and in the process began to formulate new ideas about public responsibility for the needy.

Since the mid-nineteenth century, Indiana's Township Trustees had been responsible for supporting the indigent. Before the Depression, however, the Trustees had assumed they would provide relief only to the most desperate, while city private social welfare organizations would serve the needs of others. In more prosperous times this arrangement had suited the city's private agencies just fine, including Catholic Charities, which hoped to shelter its own from the larger society. However, when private urban resources proved insufficient, the Indianapolis Council of Social Agencies, a federation of social welfare providers to which Catholic Charities belonged, called upon the Trustees to assume greater responsibility, declaring unequivocally that "the heavy load must inevitably rest on the public purse."[10] In this way the drama played out in Indianapolis mirrored other cities where the disjuncture between private resources and the needs of the unemployed compelled urban residents to reconsider the relative responsibilities of public and private bodies. As in so many cities, Catholic leaders were among the most vocal demanding greater public action.[11]

Catholic leaders hoped that the Trustees would assume greater responsibility for the poor. However, this hope was always tempered by the Trustees' notorious reputation for being stingy, a reputation confirmed repeatedly as the Depression deepened. Although the Trustees agreed in the early 1930s to accept referrals from private agencies, including Catholic Charities, these public servants dealt with the city's needs not by raising sufficient resources, but by trying to eliminate ostensible "chiselers" who, according to the Trustees, constituted a large percentage of those seeking and receiving aid. Older notions about the "worthy" and "unworthy" poor continued to dominate how local public relief agencies gave aid at a time when few were immune from economic devastation. Instead of investing resources into relief, the Trustees channeled funds into hiring additional social workers to staff the city's Central Investigation Office, a body that had responsibility for investigating new cases as well as re-evaluating older ones. In 1933, the year the city reached its all-time high unemployment rate of 37 percent, the Trustees conducted a massive reinvestigation of older relief cases, culminating in the reduction or elimination of aid to nearly 50 percent of the families they investigated. Less than 2 percent of all families actually had their allotments increased.[12] The fact that relief rolls would increase by more than 57 percent just one year later, when federal funding became available through the Federal Emergency Relief Act, suggests that the Trustees had failed miserably and that two priorities defined locally funded relief: discouraging "dependency" and keeping tax rates low.[13] Recognizing that the Trustees did "not give adequate aid," workers at Catholic Charities made public the charge that the Trustees "neglect those who should be cared for" because they "want to make a good record and have a low tax rate."[14] The Catholic community knew well that the Township Trustees, who depended on local taxes and were concerned most about appeasing the city's fiscally conservative leaders, had no incentive to contemplate let alone initiate any significant changes in the structure of relief.

Although workers at Catholic Charities complained about the Trustee system of poor relief, they had few other places to refer needy Catholics prior to the New Deal. Certainly a number of Catholics received employment through the Employment Work Committee, the city's make-work program sponsored by the mayor and the Chamber of Commerce. In many ways the Employment Work Committee was the city's most comprehensive and innovative response to the Great Depression, employing at its height close to 7,000 men. However, the program suffered from serious flaws. It provided work only to men, leaving single women to fend for themselves. Furthermore, the program was never adequately funded, and after only one month in operation the Committee stopped paying wages to the workers and instead gave them food baskets.[15]

In many states, mothers' pensions programs were expected to help widowed mothers who did not benefit from make-work programs. However, in Indiana, which created a mothers' pension program in 1920, few women ever received this aid. The public servants who oversaw the program in Indianapolis were especially stingy, granting pensions to only seventeen mothers in 1929, twenty-two in 1933, and one hundred in 1935.[16] In contrast, most northern cities, both large and mid-sized, gave pensions to a much larger number of women, measured both in real numbers and as a percentage of the population. It is impossible to know whether or not the public servants who distributed pensions in Indianapolis discriminated against Catholic women, but in a heavily Protestant city one could reasonably surmise that white Protestant women had an easier time proving their "worthiness." Statewide in Indiana, less than 1 percent of the mothers who received pensions were women of color and only $1/4$ of 1 percent had never been married.[17]

In light of the challenge workers at Catholic Charities faced as they tried to meet the growing needs of the Catholic population, it is not surprising that they began to rethink the relative responsibilities of public and private welfare agencies and became receptive to the notion that the federal government should assume a greater role in relief of the unemployed. Their receptivity was no doubt heightened when they heard Katharine Lenroot speak to them about the "trend toward public financing and public support" at the May 1933 meeting of the Indianapolis Council of Social Agencies. Lenroot, a representative from the national Children's Bureau, had come to Indianapolis to galvanize support for President Franklin Roosevelt's new Federal Emergency Relief Act, which provided federal money to states to pursue both work and direct relief. Arguing that "the social work program is no longer a matter of private funds" and "the way we provide for needs will determine whether American civilization will be a success, or go down into chaos and oblivion," Lenroot put forth a strong rationale for growing federal responsibility. Her proposition proved appealing to those in the Catholic community who saw the New Deal as an opportunity to claim a place in the mainstream of American politics.[18]

Even before Lenroot's visit, Reverend August Fussenegger, director of Catholic Charities of Indianapolis, had been exposed to the idea that government—local, state, and federal—had a moral obligation to respond to the social needs of Americans. As early as 1931, national leaders at the National Conference of Catholic Charities (NCCC) addressed the pressing question of "governmental action in the matter of direct relief and work relief." They concluded that "the largest share of the burden of local relief will be borne by tax supported funds."[19] As the 1930s progressed, Catholic leaders in Washington, D.C., including John A. Ryan and Raymond McGowan, became vocal New Deal supporters and devoted considerable energy explaining how the New Deal harmonized with Catholic social teaching. Although the conservative political sentiment in Indianapolis resisted such notions, Fussenegger brought these messages back home. After Indiana began to implement the monumental Social Security Act of 1935, he told the city's Catholics that the needs of children and the unemployed had clearly outpaced "the ability of any private agency."[20] Even more important, he proclaimed that Aid to Dependent Children (ADC) (later renamed Aid to Families with Dependent Children) was a policy "in harmony with Catholic principles and ideals."[21]

Although some Indianapolis Catholics—including Bishop Joseph Ritter—remained skeptical about the New Deal, others soon understood social welfare as a public responsibility. Writing to the *Indiana Catholic and Record,* the state's Catholic newspaper, one layman contended that the New Deal "accords with Catholic social and ethical principles and the Catholic philosophy of government."[22] As historians have pointed out, Franklin Roosevelt was one of the first presidents to embrace Catholics, and Catholics eager to prove their patriotism embraced both him and the New Deal.[23] Of course, Catholic support for the New Deal also stemmed from anti-socialist principles, as in the case of the person who wrote the *Indiana Catholic and Record* in support of unemployment insurance: "it is an intelligent move against communism" that will help "prevent social revolution."[24] Thus, the men and women at Catholic Charities in Indianapolis increasingly came to the conclusion that public social welfare programs were not only necessary but that they fit with Catholic ideals enunciated in papal encyclicals *Rerum novarum* (1891) and *Quadragesimo anno* (1931) and applied to the American context by the likes of Fathers Ryan, McGowan, and Fussenegger. Hope among national Catholic leaders that Indianapolis Catholics would follow the lead of Fussenegger and embrace the New Deal was no doubt on the minds of those who agreed that Indianapolis should host the 1937 regional meeting of the Catholic Conference on Industrial Problems (CCIP). The CCIP, established in 1922 "to promote the study and understanding of industrial problems,"[25] became a forum in the 1930s for debate about the merits of the New Deal. At the Indianapolis conference, Ryan vigorously defended New Deal minimum wage and hours legislation, declaring that "the most important opportunity before us lies in the field of legislation."[26] For men like Fussenegger, who wanted to prove that the New Deal articulated Catholic principles and that Catholics who supported the New Deal were patriotic Americans, the CCIP regional conference was crucial. In addition, in hosting the conference, the Catholic community communicated to the Protestant majority that Catholics would assume a visible public presence in Indianapolis.

Private Charities and the Emerging Welfare State

The expanded responsibilities of public agencies that administered programs such as Aid to Dependent Children and Old Age Assistance raised new questions for citizens who were urged to support private charities. Taxpaying citizens, Catholics and non-Catholics alike, who watched their government assume a greater role, wondered why they should also support private agencies. In Indianapolis the Family Welfare Society, the city's largest private nonsectarian social welfare provider, reported in 1938 that the question it had to deal with more than any other was, "Why do we need the Community Fund when we have federal relief and Social Security?"[27]

Although this question no doubt seemed logical and fair from the viewpoint of citizens trying to sort out the relative responsibilities of public and private bodies, the city's private social welfare leaders were taken by surprise. If nothing else, the private social workers' experiences with the fiscally tight Township Trustees had led them to believe that private agencies were required to supplement publicly financed work, and they assumed the general public would stand behind them. But as the general public in Indianapolis came to accept or at least tolerate a growing public presence in social welfare—and in many cases it was accepted only begrudgingly—private social workers, both secular and sectarian, found support for their services dwindling. A social worker attending the Indianapolis Conference of Social Work described the frustration of her colleagues who felt that they had "lost their purpose."[28] Ironically, then, many of the leaders of private agencies who had encouraged government at all levels to assume greater responsibility for the welfare of urban residents found that they had to resell their organizations to a tight-fisted taxpaying public.[29] As part of this effort, the private agencies belonging to the Indianapolis Council of Social Agencies decided unanimously in 1938 that the topic "public-private relations" would be the Council's theme for its meetings and outreach efforts.

How best to convince the general public of the need for private social welfare was the most important task facing private agencies in Indianapolis and in other cities across the nation. The task proved particularly daunting. Observing the national scene, historian Daniel Walkowitz found that privately employed social workers struggled to define their role and purpose within the context of an expanding welfare state. He describes how many social workers who found their pre-Depression responsibilities shifted to the public sector attempted to "reinvent" themselves: "To justify both their funding and their role, caseworkers in the private sector increasingly had to distinguish their work from that of public sector workers as less degraded and more 'professional' labor that was in the therapeutic avant-garde."[30] Although Walkowitz doubts whether privately employed social workers were any more qualified than the larger number flocking to public welfare agencies, the former believed themselves more effective and broadcast that belief to win support for their private agencies.

In conservative Indianapolis, Catholic Charities had a dual task: convincing Catholics to support both publicly funded social welfare and privately run Catholic programs. This task necessitated educating the Catholic public to the shifting boundary that separated public and private responsibilities in addition to distinguishing the particularities of each. In order to appeal to Catholics who accepted the emerging welfare state but felt less incentive to contribute to Catholic Charities, Catholic leaders highlighted the "limitations" of public social programs. "Hazards of insecurity, disease, despair, family discord and delinquency are greater dangers to temporal and spiritual welfare and require higher skills in treatment than the mere provision of physical needs."[31] In making such a claim, Catholic leaders played on the notion that privately employed social workers were, by definition, more highly skilled than their public counterparts and that Catholics had a special responsibility to look out for their coreligionists. To those Catholics who were less enthusiastic about the emerging welfare state because they feared public agencies would squeeze out Catholic programs, Catholic leaders praised the welfare state and asserted that the government had "freed [them] from the staggering burden of relief" and allowed them to focus upon the emotional and spiritual needs of underprivileged Catholics.[32]

Celebrating the virtues of Catholic Charities, Catholic social workers joined nonsectarian privately employed social workers in their attempt to distinguish their work from the publicly employed social worker. However, while nonsectarian social workers distanced themselves from religion and demonstrated their professionalism by embracing the rhetoric of science popular among university-trained social workers, Catholic social workers embraced both religion and professional social work methods. They claimed that the techniques of professional social work were compatible with Catholic principles and that only Catholic social workers could respond to the needs of other Catholics. To stem doubts about Catholic professionalism, Fussenegger made sure that Catholic Charities had the trappings of a truly "professional" agency. In 1935 he invited a professor of social work from Saint Louis University to evaluate Catholic Charities' programs, and he quickly instituted the changes she suggested. He hired more trained social workers and implemented widely recognized social work practices, such as private consultations and complete casework records.

To claim a role in the new social welfare landscape, Catholics insisted that only the Catholic social worker, schooled both in the principles of the church and the most recent social work techniques, could serve the needs of the Catholic population. As Fussenegger explained, the Catholic social worker was unique because she "brings the technical skills of the nonsectarian worker plus a deep sense of spiritual values. Hers is a religious approach based on Catholic philosophy, principles and ideals."[33] Thus, leaders differentiated Catholic social workers from both public welfare workers and private nonsectarian ones. By articulating a Catholic definition of social work and laying claim to Catholics as their special charges, Catholic social workers sought to forge a unique role as providers even while public responsibility for social welfare was growing by leaps and bounds. In contrast, nonsectarian private social workers had only their professional identities to fall back on.[34]

The New Deal and the Catholic Community

In celebrating Catholic social work, the leaders of Catholic Charities propagated the idea that public and private social welfare were qualitatively different. However, Catholic Charities hoped to do more than merely complement or parallel the expanding public welfare state. Instead, they deployed the argument that *only Catholics* could provide proper social work to *other Catholics* as a wedge to influence how publicly supported welfare operated and to make a place for themselves inside the emerging public welfare system. It was through its collaboration with the growing welfare state that the relatively small Catholic Charities of Indianapolis expanded during the 1930s, the decade when so many private welfare initiatives crumbled.

Like many of the nation's other private agencies, Catholic Charities realized early on that it could collaborate with government and even use publicly funded social programs to further its own concerns. At a time when volunteer efforts declined and resources remained scarce, Catholic Charities of Indianapolis eagerly drew on the labor of Works Project Administration (WPA) workers. Most historical discussions of the WPA understandably focus on its strengths and weaknesses as a government-sponsored make-work program. The impact the WPA had on numerous private voluntary agencies that hosted WPA workers has received little attention. Across the nation, however, WPA workers found employment at private agencies including, among others, traditional charitable organizations and social settlement houses.[35] The leaders of Catholic Charities of Indianapolis recognized that the WPA could bolster its place in the city, and Fussenegger requested WPA labor to both assist at Catholic recreational and leisure programs and build a new meeting hall. Although Fussenegger failed to get WPA help for his meeting hall project, Catholic Charities did host WPA teachers who ran recreational programs and taught homemaking, literacy, and sewing. Consequently, Catholic Charities learned that it could use the expanding public programs for its own benefit.[36] Even though conservatives complained loudly about the New Deal, the federal government's largest make-work program buttressed Indianapolis's struggling private voluntary sector.

In this regard Indianapolis was far from unique. The National Conference of Catholic Charities encouraged its agencies to make full use of WPA and National Youth Administration (NYA) workers whenever possible. NCCC even conducted an informal survey of the nation's Catholic agencies to verify that they were getting their fair share of WPA and NYA workers. When John O'Grady revealed the preliminary results of this survey at the NCCC 1936 annual meeting, he happily told the attendees that "the reports received up to this time indicate that many of the Catholic agencies are making very generous use of these governmental resources."[37]

Leaders of Catholic Charities of Indianapolis learned from their experience with the WPA that the expanding welfare state would not necessarily crowd out Catholic services and that Catholic agencies could successfully attach themselves to the new public agencies. The most important opportunity for Catholic Charities of Indianapolis to collaborate with public agencies came in 1936 when the state of Indiana passed a new welfare act. Like all states expecting to participate in the social programs the 1935 Social Security Act created, Indiana needed to construct a statewide public welfare administration. Under Indiana's new system, each county established a department of public welfare to oversee the administration of the Social Security Act's Old Age Assistance and Aid to Dependent

Children programs. These county departments also oversaw the care of children in institutions and foster care. For the first time in Indiana history, vast sums of state and local money became available for the care of children in institutions and foster homes.

Although Catholic Charities could not receive or administer funds originating from federal sources, nothing precluded it from administering state or local funds. Eager to expand their programs for children, the leaders of Catholic Charities responded to the new environment by quickly laying claim to public money, arguing that "the foster care of Catholic children whose religious heritage must be guarded and whose Catholic faith and teaching must be preserved is of vital interest to us."[38] By justifying their claims to Catholic children on religious grounds, Catholic leaders endorsed the traditional religious boundaries that had long underlay the city's social welfare system. They expected the new public welfare departments to do the same.

The story of Indiana must be placed in a larger national context. National Catholic leaders had worked hard to make sure that Catholics would retain responsibility for the care of Catholic children in the New Deal era. As historians Dorothy Brown and Elizabeth McKeown have demonstrated, the care of Catholic children had always been a central concern of Catholic providers, a concern that escalated during the New Deal. When specific provisions of the Social Security Act were being debated, Catholics were among the most vocal participants. National Catholic leaders had originally hoped that Catholic agencies would administer ADC, but having lost that battle they lobbied for ADC payments to be restricted to children cared for in their own homes by a parent or a next of kin. This restriction would necessarily leave the care of children in foster care and institutions to the individual states, where local diocesan Catholic Charities could negotiate with public welfare departments to assume responsibility for Catholic children.[39]

In addition to bending to the wishes of Catholic leaders, the framers of the Social Security Act worked hard to convince Catholics that this act would not compromise the responsibilities Catholic child-caring institutions had long claimed. In 1935, therefore,

Katharine Lenroot, one of the architects of the Social Security Act, attended the National Conference of Catholic Charities, where she assured Catholics that the "facilities provided by the Act will not relieve private agencies of any responsibility they are now carrying." She also claimed that the "strengthening of the programs and services of both public and private agencies is necessary if the needs of children are to be met."[40] Many national Catholic Charities leaders shared this belief, most notably John Butler, president of the NCCC, who in his 1936 presidential address reassured his colleagues that "Catholic efforts in this field will be increased rather than diminished."[41] To make sure that Catholics would not find themselves isolated from the growing public sector, Joseph LeBlond advised the social workers laboring at the nation's many Catholic social agencies to keep "close contact with the local public agency for administering assistance to families and children." He claimed that if they succeeded in that, "our Catholic Charities would be able to continue and extend this religious influence on an even broader scale than in the past."[42]

Reverend Fussenegger also hoped Catholic responsibility for Catholic children would grow rather than diminish with the emergence of the welfare state. Considering that Indianapolis had a smaller Catholic population and fewer resources than other large cities, this desire might have seemed naive. But Fussenegger realized that the expanding welfare state provided new opportunities for Catholic services. However, to effectively promote Catholic involvement in social welfare he needed to securely establish the right of Catholics to oversee other Catholics and to establish good relations with the public welfare authorities. Fussenegger was keenly aware that the public welfare department in Marion County had ultimate legal responsibility for all children made wards of the court in Indianapolis, but he quickly claimed the city's Catholic children as his "rightful charges" and demanded that all of the city's Catholic children in need of placement in orphanages or foster homes be sent to Catholic Charities. Fussenegger insisted that Catholic children had a right to be raised in a Catholic environment and that only Catholic social workers would be able to find suitable Catholic foster homes or run suitable Catholic orphanages. In addition, he also demanded public money for the support of these children. During his many years as director of Catholic Charities, he frequently asserted that "only a Catholic Agency can do good Catholic Social work for Catholic children and there is no reason why tax funds should not be used."[43] By making the claim that only Catholics could care adequately for needy Catholics, Fussenegger reinforced the notion that Catholics were a marginalized people who needed to protect the rights of their children. However, by demanding public money, Fussenegger also demonstrated how Catholics had developed a sense of themselves as full Americans entitled to the public dollars filling the state's coffers. Of course, the tradition of public authorities subsidizing Catholic organizations had been a common practice in New York City and other cities in the late nineteenth century.[44] But in predominantly Protestant Indianapolis, Catholics had never had such arrangements and thus the demand for public money reflected among Catholics a new understanding of citizenship. Furthermore, Catholic claims to public money won support from a wide range of Catholics, including liberals who welcomed the expanding welfare state and conservatives who held strong reservations about public programs. The former believed Catholics had a responsibility to help the expanding welfare state while the latter wanted to channel tax funds, which they saw as properly theirs, back to private bodies.

For the most part, the Marion County Department of Public Welfare complied with the demands Catholic Charities made. It referred Catholic children in need of care outside of their "natural" homes to Catholic Charities, and agreed to pay Catholic Charities for some costs it incurred through its orphanages and foster care programs. As a result, Catholic Charities expanded significantly during the 1930s, not through competition, but in collaboration with the public sector. During the decade, the number of professionally trained social workers employed by the central office of Catholic Charities increased from three to eighteen. Equally significant, Catholic Charities drew on available public funds both to expand traditional services and to initiate new ones as well.

Among the many programs benefiting from the public's largesse was the Catholic-run foster care program. Although informal Catholic foster care arrangements were not unheard of in 1929, the introduction of a large and organized foster program became possible only after large amounts of public money became available for the care of these children. Catholic Charities oversaw 218 children in 1936, a number which would rise to 330 by 1939.[45]

Other Catholic charitable programs turned to the Marion County Department of Public Welfare not to expand, but to secure sounder financial footing. For example, the Marydale Home for troubled girls, run by the Sisters of the Good Shepherd since 1873, had depended for the first sixty years of its history on private donations. Once public money became available, however, the Sisters of the Good Shepherd quickly laid claim to it. Within a couple of years the Department of Public Welfare became the Marydale's primary source of referrals and biggest financial supporter. In 1936, Marydale received financial reimbursement from the county for the care of twenty-nine of its ninety-six girls, but just two years later the court provided support for fifty-three of eighty-six girls. By 1940, just under 75 percent of the girls sent to Marydale were wards of the court and supported by public money.[46]

In addition to working closely with the Marion County Department of Public Welfare, Fussenegger established strong ties with the juvenile court. Long before the Depression, Catholic Charities had employed court workers who oversaw the care of Catholic children brought before the court. When the Juvenile Aid Division of the police department was created in 1938 to provide guidance to children before they faced serious formal charges, Catholic Charities stepped up its court work and added additional staff members to oversee proceedings. Not long after, Catholic Charities had worked out an arrangement whereby the Juvenile Aid Division had agreed to refer all Catholic children to Catholic Charities.[47] With social workers employed to do court work, the Catholic community maintained a close eye on troubled children. Once again, however, Indianapolis was not unique. Similar arrangements had originated in the nineteenth century and continued to be important in the twentieth century in cities across the nation. For example, Catholic Charities of Toledo, Ohio, had a similar working relationship with its juvenile court and boasted that it was a mistake to believe that "private agencies must decrease in number and scope of activities in the measure that public welfare increases."[48]

One of the most striking features of these new public-private collaborative endeavors in Indianapolis was the absence of Protestant participation. During the Depression, the Wheeler Mission, an evangelical Protestant organization, used WPA labor, but once the New Deal was established, it broke its ties to public authorities. No prominent Protestant organizations followed the lead of Catholic Charities in making demands on public funds. The reasons were twofold. First, in a city dominated by Protestants, Protestant agencies did not see the need to protect their own. Second, Protestants tended to maintain a more traditional view of private agencies as self-supporting.

The success with which Catholic Charities laid claim to public money raises the compelling question: Why were public welfare agencies so eager to collaborate with Catholic Charities? Even more important, why did a heavily Protestant city which two decades earlier had questioned the Catholic community's claim to the body politic, agree to channel large sums of money to Catholics? It was one thing for Protestant agencies not to demand public money, but another altogether to allow Catholics to receive it. Part of the explanation lay in the Protestant recognition that Catholics were different, and even if they were not equals, they still ought to have their own welfare institutions. Even more important, the publicly funded social welfare agencies, both the Township Trustees and the Department of Public Welfare, remained committed to keeping expenditures low and public bureaucracy small. Collaboration with Catholic Charities was one way to ensure these goals. Of course, public authorities no doubt held reservations about the Catholic community, but their commitment to fiscal conservatism proved more compelling.

Indianapolis was more fiscally conservative than most Midwestern cities. During the Depression, while Indianapolis employed more WPA workers than most all Midwestern cities, it ranked among the bottom when one examines the amount of direct relief it distributed.[49] Resistance to the "dole" continued into the late 1930s. In contrast to most other northern cities, which in the late 1930s admitted large numbers of mothers into the ADC program, Indianapolis's rolls grew only minimally, and in some years actually decreased.[50] At a time when, according to historians, close to two-thirds of all women eligible for ADC never received this aid, the city of Indianapolis celebrated the fact that it rejected more than 30 percent of its ADC applicants.[51]

The Department of Public Welfare's social workers openly admitted that they used the "suitability of the home" rather than the existence of financial need as the primary criterion when evaluating a mother's eligibility for ADC.[52] As was the case in welfare departments in so many states across the nation, "suitable home" clauses were legally incorporated into the guidelines social workers used to determine whether a mother qualified for ADC. In southern states, public welfare departments were notorious for withholding ADC from black women, who were expected to labor for low wages in the fields of white farmers. The fact that the "granting" or "withholding" of ADC could be used to reinforce racial hierarchies, regulate labor markets, and keep alive notions of the "worthy" and "unworthy" poor was not lost on Indiana's social workers. In Indiana, many social workers defined the "suitable home" narrowly to exclude unwed mothers, who by definition were viewed as morally suspect, and women of color, who were expected to support their families through their own labor. The majority of women who received ADC were white widows who conformed to the stereotype of the dependent, deserving poor. A Department of Public Welfare social worker critical of these practices complained that many of her fellow social workers used the withholding of ADC to "punish a nonconforming adult."[53]

Indiana's fiscal conservatism was even more apparent in the state's commitment to the Trustee system of poor relief. In the 1930s most states abandoned the Trustee system and handed over all poor relief responsibilities to the county departments of public welfare. Considering that Indiana's Trustee system had gained a reputation as one of the nation's most chaotic, arcane, and corrupt, it seemed logical that the state legislature should disband the system and hand over the Trustees' responsibilities to the newly formed county public welfare departments. Instead, the state legislature acceded to conservative wishes to retain the Trustee system because it allowed local communities to preserve their control over relief and ensured that expenditures would remain low.[54]

Catholic Charities in Indianapolis was instrumental in the preservation of sectarian boundaries during the New Deal and beyond. The impact of the growth of the welfare state on private agencies such as Catholic Charities in the 1930s was more complex than commonly understood. Historians of the welfare state on the national and local levels have correctly emphasized the massive shift as federal and state governments assumed greater responsibility for the needy. But the impact this shift had on private voluntary agencies is poorly understood. We know how and why many private voluntary agencies failed. Less well understood is how and why some private agencies survived and what relationship, if any, they had with the emerging welfare state.

Catholic Charities weathered the storm of the Depression not by competing with, but by harnessing itself to, the welfare state. Catholic leaders, both those who supported the welfare state and others who retained reservations about it, accepted the increase in public funds as an opportunity to expand their programs for Catholics. With public money from the Marion County Department of Public Welfare, Catholic Charities created an extensive foster care program and established a sound financial footing for its Marydale Home for troubled girls. In a city where religious divisions were strong and Catholics a minority, few in the Protestant majority questioned the right of Catholics to care for their own. For their part, public welfare authorities saw these collaborative endeavors as a means to contain the growth of public welfare and to hide its disturbing ideological implications from a conservative public. Remarkably, public funding of Catholic Charities received little public attention. This protected Catholics from adversaries who might have challenged such a relationship. It also hid how the dividing line between public and private social welfare services was blurry and dynamic, allowing Indianapolis residents to retain their Tocquevillian vision of their city as one held together by private philanthropy and voluntarism. In the 1940s and 1950s this benefited privately employed social workers who focused their attention on the middle class and justified ignoring the poor by asserting that the most disadvantaged were the responsibility of public agencies.

II

A CITY OF FAMILIES: SOCIAL WELFARE AND POSTWAR PROSPERITY

In its 1957 Annual Report, the Family Service Association (FSA), Indianapolis's largest private nonsectarian social welfare agency, highlighted one of the families that the agency's social workers had served the previous year: a married couple that "lived in a fashionable neighborhood" but "needed help with understanding and coping with" their children.[1] Anyone involved with the FSA before World War II would have noticed how this report looked very different from those issued before the war. Gone were the pleas for the wealthy to provide financial assistance to their less fortunate brethren. Instead, the FSA invited all classes, not only the poor, to take advantage of the programs it had to offer.

According to its leaders, the FSA no longer had to concern itself solely with the poor because public welfare authorities had taken over the business of relief. In the wake of New Deal social welfare programs such as Aid to Dependent Children (ADC) and Old Age Assistance (OAA), the FSA had decided that its mission was to provide social and psychological services to all urban residents, even the wealthy. These services included some that the FSA had long offered, such as care for unwed mothers and adoption. But now the FSA also gave marital/family counseling and visiting homemaking. The shift was not unique to the FSA. While the city's religiously affiliated social agencies retained a greater concern for the poor than did their secular counterparts, many of them also began directing greater attention to all classes. Some even cut their financial assistance to the poor to address social issues they believed crossed class boundaries. Together, Indianapolis's religious and nonsectarian social welfare agencies mirrored a national shift in the 1940s and 1950s, when many private agencies served a broad cross-section of their communities, not just the underprivileged.

While New Deal programs made it possible for private agencies to direct greater attention to "all classes," this does not explain why they chose to expand their reach to include all socioeconomic groups. In 1938, two years after public officials in Marion County had begun distributing ADC, the Indianapolis Community Fund remained deeply committed to the idea that the city's private social agencies should continue to focus on the less privileged and that their role within the larger welfare state was to "help prevent [their] clients from needing such assistance."[2] Leading national social workers, most notably Linton B. Swift, held out the same hope. He recognized that public welfare departments did not have the resources for intensive casework or counseling, and he expected social workers in the private sector to "supplement" the work of public agencies by providing such services to welfare recipients. By the late 1940s, however, those who urged private organizations, religious and secular alike, to find a new clientele drowned out voices like Swift's. As a result, private social welfare agencies across the nation, including many in Indianapolis, began to distance themselves from the poor in favor of serving the "entire community."

This new focus reflected and reinforced broader cultural and political changes. During the Great Depression, the economic devastation that had torn communities and families apart forced all social workers, even those trained in psychiatric social work, to address the material needs of the poor. In contrast, the booming economy that drove postwar America led many social workers and the larger public to believe class divisions were soon to become irrelevant and poverty a thing of the past. Postwar prosperity gave rise to a family-centered culture in which the image of the white middle class reigned supreme. The "norms" defined by the middle-class family, according to historian Elaine Tyler May, "represented the ideal toward which upwardly mobile Americans strove, and reflected the standard against which nonconforming individuals were judged."[3]

Social workers in search of a place in this new family-centered culture argued that they should serve all because social and psychological problems knew no class boundaries. Increasingly, then, social workers in the private sector envisioned themselves as counselors whose primary task was to attend to the psychological and social needs of families. This usually involved helping each family member "adjust" to the gender and generational roles prescribed by the celebrated middle-class family ideal.

As a result, social workers in Indianapolis and elsewhere increasingly resisted working with families that could not or would not conform to traditional gender roles whereby the father served as breadwinner and the mother tended the home. Social workers rarely spoke openly about how these gender expectations were intertwined with assumptions about class. The ideal family, defined primarily through gender, masked its class-specific nature. Consequently, while the number of middle-class families receiving assistance from social welfare agencies increased, the number of underprivileged families granted aid fell. In this way, social workers significantly defined and enforced the middle-class ideal in a society that did not like to talk about class, but which communicated class assumptions through rhetoric about gender.

These shifts transformed both secular and religious social welfare in Indianapolis. While secular social work professionals worked hard to spread the message that private agencies should serve the entire community, many mainline Protestant, Catholic, and Jewish social agencies began to speak the same language and offer similar services. Although these religious social welfare agencies still maintained their traditional concern for the poor—and in the case of Catholic Charities still received public funds—they nevertheless were attracted to the mantle of respect and authority that the new psychologically based social welfare work represented, and they sought to expand their clientele by attending to the social and psychological needs of the middle class.

Fighting for Families

Since the 1920s, most professional psychologists and social workers had accepted the idea that psychological problems could affect men and women of any social class, but it was not until World War II that the general public also embraced this belief. During wartime, citizens began to worry about the mental health of the men in the military and expressed fear that even "normal" men from upstanding families might experience psychological problems. In response, the federal government hired thousands of psychologists to screen recruits and attend to soldiers stationed both at home and abroad. The government also attempted to allay the onset of psychological problems by meeting the social needs of military men. As part of this effort, the government collaborated with religious groups such as the YMCA, the National Catholic Community Services, the Salvation Army, and the National Jewish Welfare Board. Together these private and public bodies established more than 1,800 United Service Organization (USO) community centers to provide a wide range of social and recreational activities.[4] Some Americans, including national Catholic leaders, hoped that the USOs would also offer "counsel and guidance covering the full range of personal problems."[5] While many USOs did not, an Indianapolis USO social worker noted that "an incalculable amount of personal services," including "personal counseling," was provided.[6] According to historian Susan Myers-Shirk, political officials embraced psychological testing of soldiers. As a result, "Americans came to the end of the war more willing to believe that psychological counseling could provide solutions to their problems, relieve their emotional suffering, and improve the quality of their lives."[7]

As the USOs directed attention to military personnel, civic and governmental leaders expressed concern about how the war was affecting domestic life, particularly the families disrupted by the conflict abroad. Responding to these concerns in 1943, the federal Office of Civilian Defense inaugurated Family Week to increase "family consciousness," with a special focus on "family related interests and problems within a religious context."[8] During one week in early May, all three major faiths—Catholic, Jewish, and Protestant—sponsored a variety of activities including worship services, home visiting, and parental education.

Local communities participated in these nationally sponsored events and developed their own programs as well. In Indianapolis the Community Fund, which had a long history of fund raising for private charities, warned city residents that "no free people can be healthy happy partners in this all-out war effort without the essential services by agencies supported by the Community Fund." The domestic problems, according to the Fund, were many: "desertion, separation, family breakdown," and an increase in unwed motherhood.[9] The city also had to deal with "newcomers to the community, congested living conditions, mothers taking employment, soldiers from nearby camps, [and] hasty marriages."[10] These problems arose not just in the homes of the disadvantaged, but in "thousands of homes, of all social position and economic state."[11] The Fund's leaders insisted that the city must help solve these domestic problems as part of the larger war effort because the "[men] at war must be confident their loved ones are secure at home before they can put their hearts into any fight."[12]

To fortify the home front, the Community Fund worked diligently to attend to the psychological and social needs of families left behind. The Fund's leaders hired a full-time executive to oversee social and recreational activities for Indianapolis's children.[13] The fifteen "character-building" agencies of the Community Fund, including, the YMCA, the Boy Scouts of America, and the Jewish Community Center, received special attention and supplemental funds.[14] In addition to providing more services to children, social welfare agencies attended to the needs of the parents. Social workers described with great satisfaction how "there were a large number of people, many of whom had not previously used the services of agencies, seeking casework services."[15] Social workers believed these people sought help because the "normal problems of family life were not only aggravated and intensified, but also added to by the war."[16]

Catholics, especially active in these wartime services, confidently asserted that the "family is the first line of defense." Catholic leaders established a Catholic branch of the Indianapolis USO in 1942 at 124 W. Georgia Street.[17] This particular USO took seriously its goal of creating a home-like environment, and, as part of this effort, invited girls from the local Catholic Youth Organization to attend its buffet dinners and dances, hoping they would "add a touch of gaiety to a wholesome, cheery atmosphere."[18]

The war, then, had two results. It offered social workers the opportunity to actively participate in the war effort. In so doing, it taught the public that anyone, not just the underprivileged, could seek help and advice from traditional social welfare agencies. The timing of the war proved especially propitious for those private social welfare agencies that since the New Deal had been seeking a new role and a new clientele. Of course, some private agencies, such as Catholic Charities, collaborated with the public sector and grew in large part because of their relations with the expanding welfare state. But many agencies feared they would lose their place in the city if they did not expand both the kinds of services they offered and the clientele they served. For instance, Jewish agencies organized a national conference at which they discussed their "purpose and function" and generally agreed that "people in the middle and upper brackets" had problems that traditional social agencies could help solve.[19]

A representative of the nationally based Children's Bureau summed up the new direction of social work: "Social services will no longer be identified with classes in society; the so-called dependent, neglected, defective, and delinquent. Instead they will be identified with specific human problems." These problems, she emphasized, "are no respecter of persons, of economic status, or of social rank."[20] The claim that social and psychological problems knew no economic or social boundaries represented a significant departure from the past. At first glance, it seemed social workers for the first time had abandoned classist and racist assumptions that had long underlay popular understandings of social problems such as poverty and unwed motherhood. However, the language of social service providers masked the important fact that their ideas about "normalcy" were not "declassed" but rather grounded in the gender roles and generational relations the middle-class ideal exalted.

Serving Families

In 1948, men and women from more than 125 organizations gathered at the White House Conference on Family Life. Their primary goals were to discover the "specific means by which the family may be strengthened for the benefit of its individual members and society" and to encourage social welfare agencies to develop "more family-centered concerns and family-centered programs."[21] The conference exemplified how family life figured so centrally in the culture of postwar America. Although there is no historical consensus about why the baby boom occurred, it is clear, as Elaine Tyler May explains, that Americans embraced "marriage, parenthood, and traditional gender roles."[22] The postwar baby boom not only reversed more than a century-long trend of falling birth rates, but men and women married at younger ages, and many of these young couples began having children within the first or second year of marriage.

Various forces competed with each other for the loyalty and money of these families. Most visibly, housing developers recognized the potential for massive profits in America's suburbs, and Hollywood producers helped to strengthen the particulars of the family ideal through the movies and television. Less visible but no less significant were religious authorities who gave unprecedented attention to families. Protestants, Catholics, and Jews established planning commissions to coordinate the building of new suburban churches and synagogues while the laity reinvigorated older organizations and in some cases formed new ones whose sole purpose was to attend to the needs of families. The most famous were the Catholic-affiliated Family Life Bureau and Catholic Family Life Movement, but Protestants and Jews also supported a variety of committees to encourage traditional family life.[23] In such a climate, few religious leaders listened to critics, such as the young sociologist Peter Berger, who complained, "By concentrating on the family to the exclusion of other institutions, the churches are at work not where the important decisions are made but where the effects of these decisions are passively experienced."[24]

Since social workers, both religious and nonsectarian, were certain that "most social ills have their roots in family life," they too sought to serve and "strengthen" the American family.[25] To pursue this goal, however, social workers had to define the ideal family and identify and combat forces that threatened it. The war had introduced the idea that even "normal" individuals and families, in their confrontation with the strains and stresses of modern life, could benefit from mental health professionals. In the postwar period, large numbers of ordinary middle-class Americans sought the help of psychologically trained professionals, and psychological services quickly became hot commodities for which people were willing to pay good money. As one historian explains, "Americans' expectation of a better life after the war coincided with a growing infatuation with psychiatry as a way of securing happiness."[26]

Social workers in private social welfare agencies knew that if they wanted to offer their counseling and casework services to the booming middle class, they would have to demonstrate that their agencies no longer served only the poor. In Indianapolis, the FSA worked hard to lose the "stigma" associated with service to the underprivileged. It created a special public relations committee that ran advertisements in newspapers and magazines and on radio, boldly announcing to the general public that it had evolved "from a program of service to the economically disadvantaged to a program serving the total community" and that the "problems which bring applicants to the agency have changed from those related primarily to economic need to problems arising primarily from personal and family relationships."[27] More specifically, the FSA wanted urban residents to know that "there is scarcely a home which has not felt the impact [of the war]" and that its social workers were prepared to deal with nonclass problems such as a "young couple regretting a hasty wartime marriage; a veteran who has found his job no longer satisfies him."[28]

While religiously affiliated social agencies maintained a concern for the underprivileged and even collaborated with public agencies, they too were eager to serve the growing middle class, believing that they must "reach all, not just the poor and under-privileged."[29] In 1956, the head of Jewish Social Services looked back at the decade following the war and celebrated how his organization had been "completely revitalized," transformed from a "'basket for the poor' charity into a versatile agency serving the needs of every income group."[30] Its many services included marital and family counseling, adoption, and visiting homemaking. The Social Service Department of the Church Federation—which represented hundreds of urban Protestant churches—also reached out to the middle class, distributing pamphlets to inform the city's churchgoing families of its services. One pamphlet, "So You Have Family Problems," provided information about premarital and family counseling, while another, "Our Children Have Problems Too," described resources available to middle-class parents with rebellious children. Even Catholic Charities, which offered a wide range of services to the poor, wanted to serve the middle class and publicized how its counselors dealt with problems which "might affect rich and poor alike."[31]

In general, then, religious social welfare agencies, like their secular counterparts, sought out the more prosperous classes. They provided services they thought middle-class families wanted, and they adopted the language and methods of secular psychologists who had gained so much respect during the war. As a national Jewish leader explained, "The problems brought to the Jewish family agency are for the most part of the same general nature as those coming to the nonsectarian family service."[32] The secular language proved appealing to religious providers not only because it lent an air of authority and was so widely embraced, but because it fit so well with ideas about traditional gender roles and family life that religious organizations had long embraced.

In the 1940s, a wide array of religious organizations used psychological concepts to put forward their ideas about family life. Catholics writing for the *American Catholic Sociological Review* made what one historian has described as a definite shift to a more "scientific approach to family life" without forgoing their strong commitment to traditional family configurations.[33] Catholic counseling for parents and children was noted for being "more informational than inspirational, more psychological than theological."[34] Similar trends occurred in the Protestant community. The growing popularity of psychology was especially apparent in the Family Life Clinics that were sponsored in cities across the nation, including one conducted in Indianapolis in 1942. As part of the Indianapolis Clinic, the Church Federation conducted a massive survey in which it asked more than 600 families questions dealing with various aspects of family life. What is most revealing about the survey is that Church Federation members so ably used the language of their secular counterparts, especially those in the field of psychology. For example, the survey focused on issues such as the "parent-child relationship" and "marital relations" by asking the parents how well their children obeyed them and whether or not they, the husbands and wives, had serious arguments or sexual difficulties. Other ideas and concerns popular in the field of psychology also figured prominently in the survey. In particular, the study warned about the "over-attentive" mother who risked "smothering her children."[35]

In many ways, the Church Federation survey read no differently than a secular survey. This is not to suggest, however, that there were no differences. The Clinic's participants believed that healthy families must be engaged in an active religious life. Nonetheless, the Federation's members did not use religious language to describe family problems and to prescribe solutions, turning instead to the language of secular psychologists.

The survey also clearly demonstrated the Church Federation's growing concern with middle-class families. For example, while the survey asked whether "money causes tension in our family" and how money was "provided to the children," it never inquired if families had enough money to begin with.[36] The surveyors assumed that men should be the sole providers and that they should earn a sufficient salary to allow their wives to tend to the home. Federation leaders, critical of women who worked outside the home, complained that working women not only became too independent of their husbands, but that they deprived children of their right to full-time mothers. The Church Federation supported what it called a model of "Christian Family Living" that openly and explicitly celebrated traditional gender roles and relations. As a result, the men and women who worked for the Social Service Department rarely took the issue of class seriously and focused without any qualms on serving the middle class.

The heightened attention on the middle class was not merely rhetorical. It directly and profoundly affected the services offered. Certainly throughout the late 1930s and early 1940s, most of the city's private agencies expended a large proportion of their resources on assistance to the poor. By the mid 1950s, however, agencies provided little financial assistance to their clients. The FSA, for instance, distributed relief to 46 percent of its clients in 1940, but only 13.5 percent in 1950.[37] Equally revealing, more than half of the FSA's budget in 1952 supported counseling services while only 15 percent went toward financial assistance.[38] Urban religious organizations evinced similar trends. Notwithstanding the considerable services Catholic Charities offered the underprivileged, it no longer saw relief as its responsibility, and its annual reports reminded the public that Catholic Charities "is essentially a service agency. It is not a relief giving agency."[39] Instead, Catholic leaders boasted about their new cross-class services such as "family service, domestic relations, family counseling, [and] individual counseling."[40]

Many social welfare providers shifted their resources to newer services, including marital/family counseling, visiting homemaking, unwed mother care, and adoption. In particular, counseling became especially popular. Between 1946 and 1951, the FSA more than doubled the number of people it served, most of whom received counseling. Even more dramatic increases took place at Jewish Social Services, which first introduced marital/family counseling in the postwar period and quickly made these services the agency's primary focus.[41] Catholic Charities and the Social Service Department of the Church Federation also began to give counseling sessions, redirecting funds and personnel to make sure they could offer the same programs as the city's other religious and secular social agencies.

Religious agencies were eager to attract middle-class families. To achieve this objective, they employed professionally trained social workers who used the same methods as secular providers. The Church Federation's counselors drew explicitly on the techniques employed by secular counselors when assisting couples contemplating marriage and held special group meetings at which couples discussed "all the forces that threaten family life."[42] Marian Leroy, the head caseworker at Catholic Charities, celebrated how all of the social workers at her agency had graduate degrees, explaining that "psychiatry and psychology exercised a great influence on [the] caseworkers" who use "all the skills and special knowledge of trained social workers in cooperation with pastors and the aid of modern science."[43]

A City of Families

These changes in Indianapolis mirrored the national scene. In the 1940s and 1950s, the number of social agencies offering family/marital counseling to middle-class families increased, and because religious groups had such a significant stake in the institutions of family and marriage, they were especially eager to participate. In a review of Jewish social services conducted collaboratively by Jewish leaders in Chicago, New York, Cleveland, and Baltimore, there was agreement that Jewish social agencies could serve people "hitherto not considered as the family agency clientele."[44] These Jewish leaders emphasized that the "primary emphasis" of Jewish services must be the "prevention of family breakdown, the strengthening of family ties, and the maintenance of healthy and satisfying family life."[45] In a similar way, national Catholic leaders urged their organizations to provide counseling to "ordinary, normal couples, not problem couples," and by the 1950s more than 75 percent of all dioceses nationwide offered both marital and premarital counseling, known as Cana and pre-Cana.[46] The couples who took advantage of these services were, for the most part, middle-class: 68 percent were defined as white collar and 60 percent had attended college.[47] Protestant middle-class families also flocked to their religious institutions for such help, and Protestant clergy responded by seeking training as counselors.[48]

In addition to recruiting highly educated and professionally certified staff, Indianapolis's private agencies, both secular and religious, began charging fees from some of their clients. Fee charging helped the private agencies to attract the middle class and assure this new clientele that they were not charity cases. In 1950 social workers representing the FSA told the public that they had decided to begin charging fees because "many persons refused help or advice when it came free" and that they had a responsibility to remove the "stigma of charity service which had prevented many self-supporting families from receiving help."[49] The Indianapolis Pastoral Care and Counseling Service—a Christian center—confronted the same ostensible stigma and also began charging fees to clients able to pay. Fee charging quickly became integral to the private agencies' efforts to redefine their class base.

The Good Wife

People who paid for Indianapolis's social welfare services maintained their status as middle-class citizens. The services they received reinforced assumptions about class and gender at the heart of the middle-class ideal and widely celebrated in the larger culture. For example, social workers agreed that marital discord resulted from the individual's "inability to affect an adjustment between one's own needs and the demands of the marriage," and the advice they doled out was almost always based on traditional expectations about men's and women's respective responsibilities.[50] When the *Indianapolis Star* published a story on marital counseling, the reporter interviewed a social worker who described a typical case in which a woman needed advice because her husband of twenty years was engaging in an extramarital affair. After several counseling sessions, the social worker concluded that the husband cheated because his wife had "failed to keep up her personal appearance. She had steadfastly refused to try a new type of hairdo suggested by the husband." The rival, however, "had just that type of hairdo." The counselor who had advised her client to get the "new hairstyle" and refine her "personal charm" was pleased to report that "within a week" of accepting her advice, "the husband stopped visiting the other woman, and the marriage returned to its former happy status."[51]

This example illustrates how, in the 1950s, counselors working in social welfare agencies encouraged female clients to accept, or "adjust" to, their roles as wives and mothers. Not surprisingly, women who "rejected" their femininity and attempted to assume a more masculine role were viewed as the most problematic. According to leading social work theorists, the feminine woman should exhibit seven characteristics: "pleasure in the tasks involved in making a comfortable and attractive home, enjoyment of and some natural skill in caring for her children, comfortable acceptance of financial support from her husband, a preference for staying in the home rather than working if she has young children unless work is necessary for financial reasons, the absence of a marked need to dominate or be aggressive, [and] preference for a masculine type of man."[52]

Such assumptions made it possible for the counselors at the Indianapolis FSA to tell one of their clients, a woman who had "placed great emphasis on her academic achievements," that she should not attempt either to be "accepted on an intellectual level by men" or to assume the "masculine role in the family."[53]

Even though counselors often criticized women who were too strong and independent, they also chastised those female clients whom they described as "immature, infantile, [and] excessively dependent."[54] Psychiatric social workers expressed especially strong concern for the "dependent woman" who suffered from an "unusual degree of emotional dependence" and acted like a needy child, expecting her husband to be "more affectionate, more patient, more protective, than adults usually expect."[55] The dichotomy of womanhood that social workers constructed, a dichotomy in which the "masculine woman" and "the dependent woman" occupied the ends of the continuum, served to reinforce the gender norms celebrated in the larger culture. Women were expected to locate themselves between these two extremes and could find themselves the subject of criticism if they veered too far in either direction.

Although secular social workers took the lead in defining the parameters of acceptable womanhood, Catholic social workers used many of the same concepts and methods as their secular counterparts. In Catholic pre-Cana classes, counselors taught young couples about the "differences" between men and women and the importance of adhering to traditional gender roles and upholding family life. The counselors, according to historian Jeffrey Burns, drew "frequently on the experimental social sciences, particularly sociology and psychology" and ideas such as "communication, companionship, sexual intimacy, and emotional maturity."[56] Like many secular psychologists, Catholic counselors contended that "marriages fail not because of the problems encountered but because of the inadequacies of the persons involved."[57]

Even as Catholic counselors attended to the personal bonds between men and women, Catholic social workers expressed especially strong concerns about larger societal forces that challenged family life. In particular, they were convinced that the economic prosperity that made traditional family life viable might also represent a threat to it. The postwar period witnessed a dramatic increase in the number of Catholics who could claim membership in the middle class, a status Catholics guarded even as they experienced concern about the impact it could have on Catholic identity and practice. As the executive director of Catholic Charities explained, "Under the guise of promoting an easier way of life and a release from social responsibility these detrimental forces actually eat at the very foundation of the family and society."[58] In particular, Catholics worried that women who earned high incomes might embrace the materialism of the larger culture and shirk their roles as wives and mothers. In therapy sessions, Catholic social workers worked hard to reinforce the "moral standards" that underlie family life. These concerns inspired some Catholic men and women to participate in the anti-ERA movement, especially those who believed that equal rights for women would undermine family life.

Homemaking

In addition to providing counseling services that celebrated traditional gender roles, some of Indianapolis's private social welfare agencies instituted visiting homemaking services to preserve traditional middle-class families during a temporary crisis. In the late 1940s, both the FSA and Jewish Social Services began to provide visiting homemakers to families where the mother of the household was incapable of caring for the family—usually due to illness. One agency claimed the responsibilities of the visiting homemaker were no different than the real mother. The visiting homemaker "takes over the home." She arrives in the morning to see that the children are "sent to school" and she stays until early evening when the "father comes from work." In addition to caring for the children, she prepares the husband's dinner, and the especially conscientious homemaker makes sure to arrive early enough in the morning to "prepare his breakfast."[59]

In the postwar period, visiting homemaking became popular across the nation. In some cities, social agencies used the homemakers to teach underprivileged women how to tend "properly" to their homes and families. However, in many cities, including Indianapolis, social workers saw visiting homemaking as a service for middle-class families, a service intended to help such families overcome a temporary crisis. Consider a study of twenty-nine families who received the service from the Indianapolis FSA in 1952. Twenty-five of the families were married couples and four were headed by a single parent. The four single parents included three widowed men and one single mother.[60] Of the twenty-nine families, all but three were white. The families who received the service were mostly middle- and upper-middle-class, with one of the fathers employed as a medical doctor and two as attorneys.[61] Three of the twenty-five married couples had had a paid housekeeper taking care of the children before the homemaker's services were secured.[62] In one case, the FSA provided the family a homemaker even though the mother resided in the home because the mother suffered from "acute anxiety" and her psychiatrist had recommended the service, diagnosing that "her anxiety might be relieved by the supportive relationship with a warm and giving mother figure."[63]

When agencies selected families to receive visiting homemakers, they gave priority to middle-class white families. They also carefully selected the women who served as visiting homemakers, an important task considering that the visiting homemaker was supposed to follow the established practices of the real mother instead of imposing her own. Before a homemaker would be assigned to a family, a caseworker would visit to see "what sort of home it is." The caseworker's most important concern was whether or not the homemaker could "fit with the family" and whether she shared the "same religion." It was also essential that the homemaker "know children" and "understand their behavior." Most importantly, the homemaker would need to share the middle-class background of the family because only such a woman would know how to "purchase food economically and how to manage a home." Finally, older women were preferred because they would "avoid the suspicion and jealousy of the mother."[64] Visiting homemaking was significant, not only to demonstrate how social service agencies served middle-class white families, but also to illuminate how agencies worked diligently to preserve gender roles. The homemaker devoted most of her time to the children, but her presence was valued primarily because she allowed the family to maintain a strict gendered division of labor. As one provider explained it, "the threat [of the mother's absence] lies not only in the loss of the person usually responsible for doing the household tasks but also to a much greater extent in the anxiety produced for the father when he loses his marital partner and is faced with the total responsibility of the family."[65] The visiting homemaker made sure the husband did not have to take on his wife's responsibilities and that he would retain his "accustomed way of life in his home."[66] The service enabled fathers to "maintain their homes."[67]

Of course, most agencies that provided the service did not state publicly that they were concerned more with maintaining proper gender roles than with serving children. But if care for children had been the primary purpose of the visiting homemaker, then the service would have been made available to single mothers. This was not the case. Very few single mothers had access to homemaking services. In fact, when selecting families for the homemaking programs, social workers were concerned most about "whether or not the family wants to stay together and whether it is strong enough and stable enough to be preserved as a unit."[68] Most social workers believed that "given a reasonably sound family structure, [a visiting homemaker] is a good investment in the welfare of the children; given a pathologically unsound family structure, it is a poor investment."[69] Households headed by single women were by definition pathologically unsound.

Even if single-mother households elicited little sympathy from social welfare providers, they clearly needed help. Indianapolis's three day-care centers, Lockerbie St. Nursery, Fletcher Place Community Center, and Flanner House, had a limited capacity. In 1948, Lockerbie and Fletcher together cared for only 165 children, and both had to refuse care to more than half of all parents who wanted to place their children. The women who worked at these nurseries complained that their "waiting list grows alarmingly" and that "only those most desperately in need of care are being admitted."[70]

Single women who worked outside the home were forced to find makeshift care. Some relied on family members, but a good number were compelled to leave their children unattended. A study of thirty-five working mothers conducted in 1949 revealed that at least one-quarter left their children alone, a practice that caused the women considerable grief.[71] One woman who left her children alone "locked in the house" expressed great fear for their safety because one of her boys liked to "play with fire."[72] Another woman who had four children ranging in ages from one to seven years explained that she left her children alone at home because she was "unable to make any other plan." She became so anxious about the safety of her children that she suffered a nervous breakdown.[73] African American women experienced the greatest difficulties. A domestic servant who left home at 8:00 A.M. and did not return until after 5:30 P.M. described how she was "very concerned" about her girls because her neighborhood was "not a safe one." Her worst fears were realized when some men from the neighborhood molested her daughters while she was at work.[74] The most desperate mothers placed their children in boarding homes, an especially heartbreaking solution. One such woman described how she was forced to put her children in an unlicensed boarding home and that she was able to see her children only once a week. The children cried every time she left.[75]

Although private social welfare agencies pledged to serve all families, the fact that some of the agencies devoted resources to visiting homemaking services while ignoring the needs of single mothers suggests that their primary concern was upholding middle-class family life. When doing so, however, most agencies did not speak openly about class, in large part because gender became the text through which assumptions about class were articulated and enforced. In other words, when social agencies focused on serving those families that could maintain traditional gender roles, they implicitly privileged the middle-class family over all other families for whom such gender roles were unattainable.

Serving the Community

As private agencies expanded their clientele to include the middle class, they began to determine their success rates differently than social workers had in the past. Rather than seeking to cut down their caseloads, Indianapolis's social welfare agencies saw caseload increases as proof of success. The FSA celebrated how between 1946 and 1951, it had "grown by leaps and bounds," serving 130 percent more people.[76] In 1961, the United Fund reported with enthusiasm that "almost half of the residents of Marion County in the last year have been helped by one or another agencies of the United Fund."[77] Although the Jewish Welfare Federation reached only 10 percent of all the city's Jewish families, its leaders took pride in the fact that this was "the highest percentage for cities this size."[78]

Not only had the overall number of clients increased, but the kinds of people who sought help had also changed. The recipients of assistance from the FSA in 1955 were, according to executive director Henry Graham, from "all kinds of backgrounds and from all sides of the city." He boasted how "in one week, we had four applications with Ph.D. degrees."[79] Officials at Catholic Charities reported how they too had witnessed a dramatic shift in their clientele. In 1956 "the requests for service came from individuals in practically every walk of life."[80] To reinforce its claim and reach out to the middle class, Catholic Charities included illustrations of middle-class clients in its annual reports. One of the most revealing featured a family with the father dressed in a suit and sitting in a wing-back chair, his perfectly coiffed wife standing dutifully beside him, and their children playing respectfully on the floor in front of them.

Private social welfare agencies were eager to communicate that their programs attracted prosperous, "normal" people. Did they succeed in this bid for a new middle-class clientele? National studies conducted in the 1940s and 1950s confirm their success. As early as 1945, a survey conduced in Cincinnati revealed that 75 percent of the respondents believed that social work was for "all sorts of people, including those who can pay."[81] In Milwaukee in the late 1950s, only 12 percent of the individuals receiving help from the local FSA were from the lower class, while 75 percent were classified as middle- or lower-middle-class, and 13 percent as upper-class.[82] An analysis of 260 clients of the Indianapolis FSA revealed similar trends.

Only thirty-seven depended on public assistance as their primary means of support.[83]

Private social welfare agencies eagerly filled a niche in postwar American society by meeting the psychological and social needs of middle-class families. In addition to courting the middle class, urban private social welfare organizations actively discouraged the less prosperous from seeking help. Beginning in the early 1940s, the FSA sought to restrict services to families that had demonstrated a "capacity for constructive use of casework services and for future adjustments."[84] By the end of the decade the FSA instituted this policy. When 196 people requested help from the FSA in the first two months of 1948, 106 were rejected, 75 percent of whom had "economic problems." The rejected included a forty-one-year-old mother of eight children who had been known to the agency since 1931. Social workers refused to assist her because they believed that her long history with the agency demonstrated that the agency just "couldn't help."[85] Another woman, a thirty-eight-year-old unwed mother with a four-year-old child, came to the FSA seeking aid for what the social worker classified as "an economic and housing problem." The FSA did not help her because she had "unrealistic dependency needs" and would be "unable to use case services well."[86] Both of these women belonged to a group of applicants that, according to the FSA, "had had five or more contacts with other social agencies and did not appear likely to find a satisfactory solution to their problems because of limited mental ability, strong dependency needs, very large families, and a long history of marginal income."[87] In fact, the FSA denied between one-third and one-half of all requests for help because the social workers believed that the prospective clients could not make "sufficient" use of casework. Those people seeking financial assistance were more likely to find their requests rebuffed than were those requesting psychological services.

Even the Marion County Child Guidance Clinic, a public agency that provided mental health services to children, sought to attract the middle class. Workers at the clinic were proud that most of their clients came from "moderate means, some from families of affluence; but few came from families which were economically dependent."⁸⁸ One social worker described how "the inability to conceptualize on the clinic's level is one of the factors leading to a diagnosis of non-treatment," and that "the function and purpose of psycho-therapy and/or casework as well as its vocabulary are foreign to their [poor families'] cultural milieu."⁸⁹

A national study of "in-take" policies at family service agencies revealed that Indianapolis was not unusual and that across the nation "proportionally more lower-occupational-status families terminate in consultation or referral."⁹⁰ To explain why the proportion of poor people receiving help from private agencies had declined while the proportion of middle- and upper-middle-class recipients had risen, researchers concluded that "lower-class" applicants did not accept the idea of "being helped merely by a talking process," and that social workers viewed their requests for material aid as "unrealistic expectations."⁹¹ A critic of this trend noted that social workers increasingly "look for and expect to find in the client's attitude and behaviors those norms and deviations that are characteristic of the middle class."⁹²

Unwed Mothers

As the city's social welfare agencies sought to extend their reach to the middle class and fulfill the mantra of strengthening families, they also turned to the task of limiting the number of single-parent-headed households by confronting the problem of unwed motherhood. In many ways, the unwed mother posed the greatest threat to the middle-class values that were exalted in the larger culture. Her very existence demonstrated the fragility of the middle-class ideal. Properly treated, however, the unwed mother would get psychiatric treatment, give up her child for adoption, and re-enter her family and community as if nothing had happened. In other words, social welfare agencies dealt with unwed motherhood and the threat it posed as a form of rebellion.

Unwed mothers had not always been expected to give up their children. In the 1930s, most welfare providers across the nation and in Indianapolis believed unwed mothers should keep their babies and that homes for unwed mothers must encourage these mothers to accept their responsibilities. At the Suemma Coleman Home for Indianapolis's Protestant unwed mothers, social workers forced their charges to breastfeed their babies, not only to ensure the health of the infants, but to make unwed mothers "love" their babies and want to "keep" them. Similar goals motivated women who worked at the Catholic St. Elizabeth's Home. In 1935, one social worker described how an unwed mother "didn't want to see the child," but after spending time with her baby, the mother developed a love for her child and decided to raise her.[93] Social workers at the Family Welfare Society were committed to the idea that "a mother should be helped to keep her own child and to support him, if possible."[94] In the 1930s more than 50 percent of all unwed mothers kept their children.[95]

The 1940s marked a departure from these practices. In Indianapolis as elsewhere, social workers no longer encouraged unwed mothers to keep their babies. This was true even of religious providers such as St. Elizabeth's and Suemma Coleman, both of which had a long history of viewing unwed motherhood as a chance for fallen women to redeem themselves. In the postwar period, all of Indianapolis's homes for unwed mothers encouraged mothers to place their children for adoption.

In a society that valorized the middle-class family, there was no place for the single mother. Social workers were well aware, however, that unwed motherhood was on the rise among both white and black women. According to scholar Rickie Solinger, social workers responded differently to these two groups.[96] They characterized black unwed mothers as immoral and expected black mothers to assume full responsibility for their own children. In contrast, social workers described unwed white mothers as "neurotics" who became pregnant because of psychological maladjustments. By conceptualizing black unwed motherhood as a moral problem, social workers that prided themselves as experts in psychology could ignore them. By conceptualizing white unwed motherhood as a psychological problem, social workers had a clientele to treat.

To gain support for their new approach to white unwed motherhood, social workers needed to spread the message that unwed motherhood "doesn't honor class, rank or income. Its shadow will fall on the sub-deb as readily as on the well-digger's daughter."[97] Communicating through a wide array of public mediums, social workers broadcast that the white unwed mother was not usually the promiscuous girl from "across the tracks," but rather the "girl next door 'type.'"[98] Social workers believed that the truly promiscuous girls knew how to prevent pregnancy and that it was the naive girl, the girl with "limited knowledge of sex," who got pregnant.[99]

If social workers rejected the idea that white unwed motherhood resulted from an internal immorality, then how did they explain it? Whether they worked in religious or secular agencies, most social workers agreed that pregnancy was merely "symptomatic of a personality problem." Some believed that the unwed mother was led by a "purposeful, but unconscious, drive to have a baby out of wedlock as an outlet for, or a temporary solution to, an inner problem." This might include acting out a "deep-seated need of love and demonstrated affection." It might also be an attempt by the girls to "'repay' their parents for real or imagined injustices."[100] The head of Lutheran Child Welfare suspected that "in most cases there has been evidence of a poor relationship between the unwed mother and her own mother."[101] In this way, the mother was "responsible for the daughter's illegitimate motherhood in most cases, exercising too loose or too firm control."[102]

By describing unwed pregnancy as a form of rebellion, which more often than not was unconscious rather than conscious, social workers had a new clientele to treat. Maternity homes that had previously served the working class shifted gears and began focusing on the middle class. Suemma Coleman Home achieved this transition by instituting a selective admissions policy. Social workers admitted only those girls who "will get along well with the group." They refused admission to girls who were "lower in educational attainment" or who lacked "intelligence," arguing that those kinds of girls would be "ostracized by the group."[103] St. Elizabeth's was not as open as Suemma Coleman about its admission guidelines, but because of the large fees it charged ($250 in 1955), it guaranteed that only the middle class would have access to its home. Furthermore, neither served black unwed mothers.[104]

The white middle-class girls who received assistance from the city's maternity homes were expected to both give up their children for adoption and confront the psychological problems that had led them to get pregnant in the first place. There were, of course, a number of girls and women who did not want to give up their children. A social worker at the Indiana Girls' School reported that at her school "the majority of their girls feel there is nothing morally wrong with having a baby out of wedlock. The wrongdoing, they feel, is in giving the baby away."[105] This was true also of some of the girls seeking help from the Suemma Coleman Home. In 1955, the home's director, Ruth Henderson, described how "many girls coming to the home early in their pregnancy have sometimes felt a desire to keep their children." According to Henderson, maternity homes had a responsibility to discourage girls from keeping their babies, and she happily reported that most mothers will "change their minds with a closer review of the physical requirements such an arrangement would demand."[106] At Catholic Charities, Reverend Fussenegger assumed the same role. He "paints for them a picture of the future—how things will be if they decide to keep their child," always emphasizing the "thorny path" the women would face. At Lutheran Child Welfare, social workers told stories to its unwed mothers about other unwed mothers who had initially kept their babies only to give them up later, "causing emotional problems for the children."[107]

Most social workers believed that "a girl wishing to keep her out-of-wedlock baby is prone to think only of caring for a cuddly infant, like a doll." They informed the young women that the fact they had gotten pregnant demonstrated that they were incapable of becoming good mothers.[108] There were no exceptions, even for older women. When, for example, a twenty-eight-year-old woman named Mary sought help at Suemma Coleman, she expressed a desire to keep her baby, explaining that because of her age she feared she "might not have another child."[109] But she, like the other girls and women, was told that she could not possibly fulfill the requirements of motherhood. As a result of the pressure placed on these unwed mothers, they were more likely to give up their children for adoption than mothers who received no assistance from maternity homes.

The postwar shift in treatment for unwed mothers demonstrates that there was no room for those who deviated from widely celebrated cultural norms. As might be expected, homes for unwed mothers judged their success by the number of clients who gave up their children for adoption. Unlike the 1930s, when at least 50 percent of all unwed mothers kept their children, in the 1950s considerably fewer women retained custody of their children. For example, between 1958 and 1960, Suemma Coleman cared for a total of 116 girls, 88 of whom gave up their babies for adoption.[110] St. Elizabeth's reported similar numbers. In 1960, 72 of the 95 girls who received assistance relinquished custody of their children.[111]

Social workers celebrated this trend, secure in their belief that adoption benefited both mother and child; it gave the mother a chance to "rebuild her life and marry," while it offered the child a chance to live in a normal home.[112] In other words, adoption provided an opportunity for all persons involved to assimilate into mainstream society. It also provided an opportunity for social welfare providers, through adoption services, to work for the middle class. Catholic Charities frequently highlighted its adoption services in its annual reports, and the Church Federation organized special gatherings where prospective parents could learn about adoption opportunities. One such meeting in 1949 attracted more than 174 people from forty-six churches.[113] As a result, the demand for children often outpaced the available babies, and adoption agencies instituted selective, class-based adoption standards. At Catholic Charities, for example, prospective families were required to be able to provide the child with a "room of his own."[114]

The Underprivileged

As private social welfare agencies became concerned with the middle class, who served the poor, traditionally the primary clientele of social agencies? How did social workers' middle-class ideals affect their interactions with the poor? Catholics and mainline Protestants worked diligently to reach the middle class, but they also continued to provide social services to the less privileged. They were optimistic about their chances for success with the poor, in large part because they focused so much of their attention on children.

Even though many private agencies lost interest in the underprivileged adult population—who, according to the larger culture, should support themselves—the agencies expressed concern for the children of the underprivileged as victims of irresponsible parents. For instances, Catholic Charities had an extensive foster care program and homes for troubled girls and boys, and they exercised oversight for children in the juvenile court. Mainline Protestants also focused primarily on children, including Fletcher Place Community Center and Mayer Chapel, two institutions that closely resembled early-twentieth-century settlement houses. Located in poor neighborhoods, these Protestant institutions provided children with a variety of social and recreational activities, all of which were devoted to reforming their characters.

These men and women who labored at the mainline Protestant and Catholic institutions were eager to demonstrate that they were familiar with the latest advances in psychology and social work and that these approaches could be applied not just to the middle class but also to the poor. This explains their abiding concern for the underprivileged when other social welfare organizations ignored the poor. For example, when Fletcher Place Community Center expanded its health and leisure activities among the poor population on the south side of Indianapolis in 1951, the director warned, "When a church lacks wisdom and insight into social service techniques, it is blind."[115] In fact, the women who worked at Fletcher Place sounded no different than their secular counterparts. They pointed out the beneficial "personality changes" that the troubled children at their center had undergone.[116] Catholic social workers also turned to the language and methods of secular workers, voicing their concerns about whether poor children were "maladjusted." Clearly, agencies that provided for the underprivileged recognized the need to be a part of the larger social work world in which psychological explanations of social ills trumped environmental and structural critiques.

Among religious groups, only evangelical Christians rejected wholesale the psychology-based social work that had become mainstream. Evangelicals instead claimed that the downtrodden would become productive citizens only if and when they accepted Jesus

Christ as their personal savior. Focusing on the adult population, the city's evangelicals ran all Indianapolis homeless shelters, with the primary purpose of saving souls. Although optimistic about their abilities to evangelize, they remained skeptical about the men who sought shelter. Their urban missions developed punitive practices, limiting the nights each man could seek shelter and forcing men to stand while they ate their meals. According to Wheeler Mission's director Ruben Merton, the mission had to limit the amount of time the men stayed or risk "harboring parasites."[117] These practices should not be surprising considering that homeless men existed outside the bounds of acceptable society. Not only had they failed to support their families, they had failed even to support themselves. At a time when many secular and religious social workers carefully selected their clientele—accepting only those who would be able to make good use of casework—evangelical Christians hoped to convert the most desperate.

Public welfare authorities also were responsible for assisting the poorest members of society, most importantly unwed mothers. But their treatment of unwed mothers demonstrates that public officials worked to maintain the same gender and class ideals so central to private social welfare agencies. As early as the 1930s, conservative public welfare officials concerned about the cost of supporting illegitimate babies encouraged unwed mothers to give up their babies for adoption and discouraged them from seeking public assistance. In Indianapolis, a fiscally conservative city, few women received public assistance of any kind, and most of these women were white widows. Public authorities did not want to provide assistance to unwed mothers—either black or white—whom they described as "illicit." This created especially troublesome conditions for African American women who, as a rule, were excluded from most private agencies and did not have the option of placing their children for adoption.

In national circles, Indianapolis public welfare workers were noted for being "unsympathetic toward the unsuccessful and punitive toward the nonconforming."[118] In 1948, 904 women applied for ADC, but only 562 applications were approved. Even though women with dependent children were legally entitled to ADC, social workers often told needy women that they must first try to "seek employment" because they "would be much happier earning [their] own money than getting assistance."[119] Caseworkers also frequently failed to inform women of their right to food stamps, and, as a result, only 19 percent of ADC clients received food stamps in 1942.[120] Those women who did receive assistance were closely "scrutinized" and, according to one critic, forced into a "subordinate position."[121]

Poor mothers who sought public assistance risked more than rejected applications and humiliation. Their very right to raise their children was challenged. In 1945 the Indiana state legislature made it mandatory for all public welfare authorities to identify for the juvenile courts women who bore additional children while receiving ADC. The juvenile judge had the power to make the children of such families wards of the court. Women who were struggling to make ends meet could lose custody of their children if they sought public support for them.[122] These threats weighed especially heavy on African American women, who bore much of the public's hostility toward public assistance.

Fearing the punitive practices of the public welfare office, most women attempted "to manage alone or by some other means before seeking assistance."[123] The punitive practices of the public welfare authorities, the state legislature, and the courts made it extremely difficult for single mothers to provide the kind of full-time parenting that middle-class mothers were not only expected to give but were praised for giving. Unwed single mothers were in an untenable position. While criticized for their failure to live according to the middle-class ideal, they were chastised when they attempted to receive the public assistance that would have allowed them to be full-time mothers. Clearly, these practices demonstrate that many social workers adhered to a class hierarchy that valorized a white, middle-class ideal unattainable by so many.

In the 1940s and 1950s, many private social welfare workers argued that social ills knew no class boundaries and that they had a responsibility to serve the "entire community." Drawn to the authority that psychologically based social work represented, many religious social welfare providers followed the lead of their secular counterparts when they employed the same language, expressed the same goals, and focused on the same clientele. Yet even as social agencies expanded their reach to include "all classes," many agencies focused primarily or only on those families who could conform to traditional gender roles or whose problems could be "counseled away." Family/marital counseling, care for unwed mothers, and adoption services—which together made up the central activities of many private social welfare agencies—served to buttress the white, middle-class family ideal cherished in the larger culture. Ironically, the social welfare agencies that claimed to reach "all" not only ignored the poor but guaranteed that pervasive American economic divisions remained unchallenged.

Changes in social welfare in the 1940s and 1950s had roots in the 1930s, when public welfare authorities increasingly took over the business of relief. In response, many private social welfare agencies felt compelled to redefine their mission and scope, deciding to reach out to all classes rather than just the poor. The popularity of this approach transformed many religious organizations. Even though they maintained a concern for the poor, they also sought to serve the middle class. These religious organizations frequently used the language and methods of secular social workers and psychologists, who had helped define and enforce the middle-class ideal at the center of the nation's cultural life. Not until the 1960s would the nation's social workers begin to re-evaluate the missions of their agencies.

III

REDISCOVERING POVERTY, REDEFINING COMMUNITY: RELIGION, THE CIVIL RIGHTS MOVEMENT, AND THE WAR ON POVERTY

In the summer of 1965, the executive committee of Community Action Against Poverty (CAAP) decided to establish Indianapolis's first federally funded neighborhood center (called community action agencies in most cities) at St. Rita's Catholic Church, an African American church located in Martindale, one of the city's poorest neighborhoods. In the days that followed, the news media described how St. Rita's was a good choice to house what became known as the Martindale Area Citizens Service (MACS), because the parish had already demonstrated a strong commitment to the city's underprivileged, offering a wide array of social services from emergency aid to day nursery care. When Faye Williams, the church's most active parishioner, agreed to lead the new neighborhood center, it seemed that St. Rita's was ready to fight Indianapolis's War on Poverty.[1]

Notwithstanding the joy generated at the opening of the neighborhood center at St. Rita's, conflicts raged for control of the War on Poverty and over the battles its warriors should fight. In Indianapolis and in cities across the nation, conflicts became particularly intense surrounding this federal initiative that included an assortment of loosely affiliated programs with competing missions. For example, the War on Poverty funded Head Start (preschool education) and Manpower (employment training), both of which used education to fight poverty on an individual basis. However, other programs, such as the Community Action Programs (which funded the neighborhood centers) and the Legal Services Organization (LSO), were based in part on the assumption that poverty should be attacked by empowering the poor to challenge and reform the political structures which had left so many behind. These more innovative programs marked a significant departure in the history of social welfare, raising important questions about what specific rights and opportunities were needed to create a truly democratic society.

The War on Poverty also provoked conflicts over the meaning and practice of local control. The Office of Economic Opportunity (OEO), the federal agency that oversaw the War on Poverty, sought to include the poor on the local level not merely as program recipients but as program administrators, as mandated through the "maximum feasible participation" clause in the federal legislation. In practice, the "maximum feasible participation" clause was supposed to ensure that each city that received federal funds would allow poor people to sit on the local poverty boards responsible for developing and overseeing programs. Across the nation the poor took this opportunity to challenge the paternalistic attitudes of traditional social welfare providers. Poor people argued that social welfare programs should challenge class and racial inequalities and expand the rights of citizenship. This put them on a collision course with traditional social welfare providers and conservative politicians who hoped to use the War on Poverty and the rhetoric of local control to further their own interests and monopoly over social welfare.[2]

In Indianapolis, African Americans quickly emerged as the most vocal participants in the debates surrounding the War on Poverty, as they sought to use this new initiative as a means to challenge a painful history of inequality. Constituting 21 percent of the city's population, African Americans had long expressed frustration with discrimination in Indianapolis.[3] In the 1960s, most African Americans lived in one of two sections of the city: Martindale on the east side and the Indiana Avenue corridor just northwest of downtown, where most black businesses were located and the city's only public housing project stood. Poor whites with roots in the Appalachian south populated neighborhoods south of downtown. Affluent whites, people with cultural roots in the North rather than the South, resided north of 38th Street, the boundary between Indianapolis and its northern suburbs. African Americans were, quite literally, sandwiched between these two distinct communities, and the forms of segregation they faced reflected the mix of northern and southern values expressed in the geographic layout of the city. Although African Americans in Indianapolis did not face the elaborate segregation laws that ruled in the South, discrimination and segregation nonetheless defined their daily life, determining where they worked, lived, and went to school. Businesses openly discriminated in their hiring practices, with the result that in 1960 the medium income for the black population was $4,378, approximately 30 percent less than the overall city average of $6,100. The black unemployment rate of 7.6 percent exceeded the city rate of 4.5 percent. Blacks did not fare any better in Indianapolis's housing market. In black neighborhoods, 35 percent of the housing was defined as dilapidated or deteriorated, in contrast to 19 percent citywide.[4] Early in life, black school children who attended all-black schools learned that the dominant white community viewed them as an inferior population from whom whites needed to remain separate.

African Americans had struggled after World War II for antidiscrimination laws in the fields of education, employment, and housing. However, the legislation passed was usually too weak to have an impact. For example, the state passed its first school desegregation law in 1949, but segregation was still widespread in the 1960s, prompting federal intervention.[5] Similarly, Indiana's fair employment law of 1945 remained ineffective in large part because it was a voluntary measure lacking enforcement powers.[6] As a result, blacks not only earned less than whites but they also found entrance to higher-paying jobs closed. Finally, in the 1960s both the Democratic and Republican parties resisted an "open housing law" which would have made it illegal for home sellers to discriminate by race, assuring the segregation of African Americans into all-black neighborhoods. Both political parties defended their position on the grounds that the legislation interfered with the "rights" of sellers.[7]

Indianapolis was a city divided geographically and racially, whose African American residents figured disproportionately among the poor. As such, when the War on Poverty officially arrived in Indianapolis in 1965, African Americans involved in the civil rights movement recognized an opportunity to both participate in the formal policy-making arena and challenge racial boundaries and inequalities. Led by their outspoken clergy and a small number of sympathetic whites, African Americans sought to democratize the social welfare system and its political networks. They invoked the federal mandate for "maximum feasible participation" as a legal wedge to expand their economic and political rights. African American leaders insisted that the neighborhood centers must be left in the hands of local residents, and that African Americans must be actively involved in all War on Poverty programs and the local CAAP board overseeing them. African Americans also embraced the federal OEO's recommendation that communities create non-profit organizations to direct War on Poverty programs as a way to democratize social welfare and eschew dependence upon established governmental agencies. For the first time, African Americans nurtured hopes that social welfare would confront racism and class inequality and extend full rights of citizenship to all urban residents.

Yet as African Americans tried to use the War on Poverty as a vehicle to define and achieve full rights of citizenship, they had to battle Indianapolis politicians who wanted to integrate the War on Poverty into the city's existing political and social networks. John Barton, the Democratic mayor, and William Stanton, the head of the Marion County Department of Public Welfare, resisted African American leaders. They preferred a uniquely Hoosier version of the War on Poverty that would reinforce the paternalism that had long defined both Indianapolis's private and public social welfare systems. Although Barton accepted federal resources, he had faith that the city could maintain its tradition of "Hoosier independence."

For Indianapolis, the "northernmost southern city," Hoosier independence meant, quite simply, traditional elite control.

This chapter examines how the War on Poverty unfolded in Indianapolis between 1965 and 1968. After an analysis of the storm that followed Mayor Barton's decision to place the city's traditional elite on the CAAP board, I discuss War on Poverty programs themselves and the controversies they stimulated within the CAAP board. The political rift that finally tore the board apart forced federal government intervention in 1968. Through careful attention to the local flow of events, I hope to demonstrate that the War on Poverty in Indianapolis, although affected by larger social forces, was not determined solely by them. Furthermore, the chapter addresses historiographical issues by building a bridge between the history of the War on Poverty and the histories of urban religion and the civil rights movement. While historians have explored connections between the War on Poverty and the civil rights movement[8] and the role of religion in civil rights,[9] the interconnections among all three—urban religion, the War on Poverty, and the civil rights movement—have not received much attention. In Indianapolis and in other cities, these three were tightly interwoven.[10]

The Hoosier War on Poverty

In the early spring of 1965, Mayor John Barton announced that Indianapolis would join the War on Poverty. Federal funds would be used to establish a nonprofit agency, CAAP, to oversee a wide array of programs, including educational and employment initiatives such as Head Start, the National Youth Corps, and Manpower, as well as more innovative community-based initiatives such as the neighborhood centers and a Legal Services Organization. Indianapolis's choice to accept federal money was in and of itself significant because the city had always prided itself on rejecting most forms of federal aid, believing autonomy from the federal government was necessary for maintaining Hoosier independence. However, Barton had been elected in 1964 on the promise that he would seek federal funding for a variety of purposes, including highway construction and urban renewal. With the federal government's promise to fund 90 percent of the costs of the War on Poverty, it was an initiative hard to pass over.

Barton was aware, of course, that the federal government expected the poor themselves to help design and administer the War on Poverty. Like other mayors in large cities, Barton had to balance this federal mission with the interests of local political authorities and traditional social welfare providers. It soon became clear Barton expected the War on Poverty to operate like a "traditional" social service program, a goal he hoped to achieve by integrating the new programs into the city's long-standing social and political networks. As such, Barton relinquished control of key War on Poverty programs to traditional social service and educational providers. For example, Head Start and the National Youth Corps were handed over to the Indianapolis School Board. Barton appointed the city's most powerful people to the CAAP seven-member executive committee, which had ultimate responsibility to plan and administer all War on Poverty programs and which would preside over the larger forty-member CAAP board. The seven original members included Frank Meech (administrative assistant to Barton), Richard Lugar (Indianapolis School Board member), Carl Dortch (executive vice-president of the Chamber of Commerce), Bruce L. Weber (county commissioner), John VanBeten (representative of the County Health and Hospital Corporation), Howard E. Gustafson (director of Community Services Council), and David D. Smith (member of the AFL-CIO).[11]

Barton's expectation that traditional authorities would exercise control over the War on Poverty was not surprising. Few in the city had ever successfully questioned elite control of social welfare. Although Indianapolis's largest religious minority, the Catholics, had long demanded public resources in their quest to care for "their own," their requests had never posed a threat to the city's larger social welfare structure. In contrast, the federal mandate for "maximum feasible participation" of the poor represented a significant threat to the city's social welfare system. Like Democratic mayors in other northern cities, Barton attempted to fit the War on Poverty into his city's political structure. He needed to look no further than

Chicago for a successful example. Richard Daley, Chicago's Democratic mayor, not only ignored the legal mandate for "maximum feasible participation" of the poor in the decision-making process, he gained complete control over the War on Poverty in Chicago by integrating its programs into his political machine.[12]

Barton's hope for complete control over CAAP was short-lived. As soon as the mayor announced his plans in April 1965, he found himself mired in a storm that swept over Indianapolis for the next two months. Clergy who had extensive involvement with the poor mounted protests against Barton's CAAP appointees and argued that he had undermined the spirit and purpose of the War on Poverty. No group spoke out more loudly than the clergy in the Christian Inner City Association (CICA). Soon after the mayor announced his appointees, members of the CICA organized a press conference at which they lambasted the mayor's choices and questioned why the board was not democratically elected. Miller Newton, the white, twenty-six-year-old president of the CICA and minister at Fletcher Place Community Center, led the charge. Newton asserted that the executive committee "is clearly illegal because it was not elected . . . and does not include anyone from the $3,000-and-under income group." Newton felt strongly that "the poverty groups should have an equal footing on the board with members from the power structure" and that to do otherwise would be a travesty because "this is the whole idea of the President's anti-poverty program."[13] When a member of the Chamber of Commerce received an appointment to the executive committee, Newton pointed out the irony that "our Chamber of Commerce for years has resented the federal government telling it what to do with federal funds and then, all of a sudden, it gets a federal grant and it wants to tell the poverty group what to do."[14]

That Newton, president of the CICA, assumed such a critical role was not surprising. Founded in 1963, the CICA, an ecumenical group, attracted white and black clergy and forcefully advocated for the urban poor.[15] Before the War on Poverty, the CICA had lobbied for public housing and had worked to expand the electorate to include even the most deprived. The CICA had also called for raising the minimum wage and ending racial discrimination in education. At the heart of CICA activities stood the commitment to assist the underprivileged to "exercise their rights as citizens."[16] Most importantly, its members argued that access to decent housing and a living wage constituted social rights of citizenship that were no less important than long-venerated political ones.

Because of their extensive contact with Indianapolis's political and social welfare networks, CICA members had no doubt that the War on Poverty would fail if it were integrated into those networks. In particular, the CICA was convinced that neither the Department of Public Welfare nor the Township Trustees—the main governmental agencies responsible for public assistance—could deal fairly or effectively with the poor. The former was stingy and intolerant, the CICA charged, while the latter was stingy and incompetent. CICA leaders argued that if the mayor merely integrated the War on Poverty into the city's traditional social welfare structure—a structure that left the poor out of positions of power—the program would become another form of "welfare colonialism."[17] The CICA's use of the term "colonialism" demonstrated all too clearly that its members believed the traditional welfare authorities reinforced class and racial divisions and, as a result, limited the rights of citizens. CICA members expressed great enthusiasm for the War on Poverty precisely because they saw it as an opportunity to press forward a new conceptualization of citizenship that included basic social rights, like access to adequate housing and competent legal representation, as well as civil rights.

In taking such a prominent role in local discussions about the War on Poverty, the CICA joined a host of other religious organizations across the nation. In heavily Catholic cities, diocesan officials drew on the social teachings of the Catholic Church, which spelled out that basic social needs should not be left solely to charities but must also be met by government, to articulate their vision of a just War on Poverty. Believing Catholics could play an important role in the administration of the War on Poverty, Catholic leaders encouraged their parishioners to take an active role. In 1968 alone, Catholic-affiliated nonprofit organizations in fifty-five cities received more than twenty-one million dollars from the federal government to administer various War on Poverty programs including

Head Start classes, National Youth Corps, and community action programs.[18] Not atypical was the Philadelphia archdiocese's "Operation Discovery," an after-school reading program.[19] In dozens of other cities, Catholic leaders participated in War on Poverty programs without themselves directly receiving or administering money. They did so by inviting local neighborhood residents to conduct War on Poverty programs in their churches, by volunteering their own labor, and by providing much-needed knowledge of the surrounding neighborhoods to those seeking information. These religiously affiliated nonprofits reached more than 200,000 people in 1967 alone.[20]

Most of this activity took place in the North, but it was in Mississippi where the Catholic Church became most heavily involved in the War on Poverty. The federal government awarded Operation Star—a Mississippi-based nonprofit established by the Catholic Church—more than five million dollars, recognizing that local political authorities left unchecked would impose the South's racial system on War on Poverty programs. In contrast, in Indianapolis the Catholic hierarchy did not become active spokespersons in the debates surrounding the War on Poverty even though individual clergy and a small number of parishes were actively involved in War on Poverty initiatives.

Regardless of what specific religious groups joined the War on Poverty, across the nation African Americans believed that the War on Poverty provided a means to realize their search for full rights of citizenship.[21] Although its racial system was not as repressive as those in the Deep South, Indianapolis had long denied African Americans full rights of citizenship. African Americans saw the mayor's co-optation of the War on Poverty as another example of the marginalization of African Americans. Reverend Andrew J. Brown, pastor of St. John Baptist Church, was one of the first to describe the War on Poverty as a civil rights issue. Born in Mississippi and raised in Chicago, Brown arrived in Indianapolis in the late 1940s after graduating from the Moody Bible Institute. He quickly gained a reputation as one of the city's foremost civil rights leaders, using his pulpit to demand that the city end its discriminatory practices. In the 1960s, he became active in a large number of civil rights organizations, including the Southern Christian Leadership Conference (SCLC) and the Indianapolis Social Action Council. He also became one of Mayor Barton's harshest critics, constantly pointing out problems with CAAP. Like his colleague Reverend Newton, Reverend Brown was disturbed by the fact that the CAAP executive committee included no representatives of the poor and, as such, had violated the federal mandate. Instead, according to Brown, the executive committee included "the very people who have been known to cause some of the problems we have."[22]

Equally disturbing to Brown, the committee included only one African American, David Smith, a member of the AFL-CIO. Brown and other African American civic leaders complained that he "was unknown to local leaders and has never been active in any civic or civil rights causes here in Indianapolis."[23] Reporters for the *Indianapolis Recorder*, the city's African American paper, asserted that the mayor had "ignore[d] a wealth of qualified Negroes who are serving this community and instead picked a man who would not upset the status quo."[24]

For Reverend Brown and other African American leaders who viewed the War on Poverty as an opportunity to become involved in key policy-making decisions, the appointment of David Smith represented a big setback and did not portend well for the future. Brown responded publicly by demanding, "We want Negroes on these committees. We want Negroes who know the people and who through living and working with these people know the needs of these areas to be embraced by the anti-poverty program."[25] His words resonated among a population that had never been fully accepted in the city's political arena.

The battle over the War on Poverty invigorated the civil rights movement in Indianapolis, which had not been strong in comparison to movements in other northern cities. For example, the local NAACP, incensed over the executive committee appointed by Barton, "released a withering barrage at the Mayor" and threatened to both "contact the Washington office of the OEO and to seek an injunction."[26] Equally important, the local chapter of the SCLC, of which Reverend Brown was the head, voiced similar complaints. Reverend C. L. Vivian, an associate of Martin Luther King who was in Indianapolis in the spring of 1965 to help establish a local SCLC chapter, was deeply disturbed at the mayor's control of CAAP. Vivian wanted the congregations he addressed to understand that even though African Americans in Indianapolis did not suffer the magnitude of violence suffered by those in the South, they nonetheless faced "a power structure that by gentlemen's agreement leaves the Negro out of good housing, jobs and education."[27]

The controversy over Barton's control of the CAAP gave the nascent local SCLC an issue around which to organize and helped Indianapolis's African Americans see the implications of economic issues for civil rights. In this spirit, at a celebration of the founding of the new SCLC chapter, the SCLC vice president proclaimed that "this revolution has reached a point where it can no longer be confined to the South. We in the North have emerged into the economic phase of the conflict, which is the basic phase. The masses of the North are suffering from economic discrimination." He warned his audience that these issues would not be addressed should the city allow the War on Poverty to remain in the hands of the "economic overlords in the suburbs."[28]

Believing Barton's control over the CAAP was a violation of democratic principles generally and the law specifically, Reverend Brown sought support from national leaders, whom he expected to intervene on behalf of the African American community. In the spring of 1965, Brown traveled to Washington, D.C., where he spoke with black congressman Adam Clayton Powell from New York, chairman of the House Education and Labor Committee. Brown complained that neither the poor nor representatives of the poor had been included on the CAAP board or its executive committee. He singled out as especially troubling Barton's decision to back Paul G. Barker as executive director of CAAP. Although Brown did not question Barker's talents, he expressed grave concern that Barker, a white man, knew little about the African American community and that he had never been involved in issues relating to poverty. Brown explained, "70 percent of the people who will benefit from the local anti-poverty effort are Negro" and "there is an approach to the Negro problems which can only be handled through Negro leadership."²⁹ Ironically, then, Brown's claim for African Americans' involvement in the War on Poverty was legitimized by the fact that the city's poor whites, most of whom had roots in the Appalachian South, wanted nothing to do with CAAP because they "see it as a program for the 'colored.' "³⁰

Beyond the fact that Barker was white and had no experience with poverty, Brown was also bothered by rumors that surrounded Barker's hiring. Many African Americans believed that "before any applicants were interviewed, Barker had been promised the job."³¹ Although this cannot be determined, for African Americans who had been excluded from formal politics, this scandal offered further evidence of the undemocratic nature of the city.

In an effort to expand community participation in the War on Poverty, Reverend Newton also traveled to Washington in the spring of 1965 to publicize the fact that CAAP would remain undemocratic and unlawful without federal intervention. As a representative of the CICA, Newton met with Andrew Jacobs, Jr., Indiana congressman, and Robert Williams, regional consultant for the OEO. Although no records of these meetings exist, Newton no doubt explained that the CAAP board and its executive committee had violated the legal mandate for the "maximum feasible participation" of the poor.

When Brown and Newton argued for federal intervention to make certain the poor participated on the CAAP board, they rejected Indianapolis's tradition of "Hoosier independence" and articulated a new definition of citizenship. Their understanding of the rights of citizenship was informed in large part by the precepts of justice that grew out of their faith. They were not unique, for across the nation religious communities felt a moral obligation to speak out in support of the War on Poverty. This was especially true of the Interreligious Committee Against Poverty. A national consortium of Jews, Catholics, and Protestants who joined forces in 1965 to present a unified voice to encourage religious organizations to participate in the War on Poverty, the Interreligious Committee demanded that Congress provide more funds for this unprecedented federal initiative. When Congress debated funding for the War on Poverty in 1967, the Interreligious Committee's leaders wrote strong letters of support to President Lyndon Johnson and demanded before the Congressional Committee on Education and Labor that Americans "dedicate ourselves to the creation of that equitable society which is the only real answer to social unrest and injustice."[32] The Interreligious Committee understood the War on Poverty to be more than a social service program. It believed that the federal initiative provided an opportunity to examine and confront larger inequalities.

Newton's high hopes that the War on Poverty in Indianapolis would serve to democratize the city's social welfare system led him to complain that "when the program finally got here, someone else took it away from us."[33] Newton was speaking of Mayor Barton. In a city known for its social and political conservatism, Newton worked tirelessly, reminding the public that "the Economic Opportunity Act of 1964 mandates that those to be served by its programs must have an effective voice in the creation and administration of those programs."[34] Toward this end, he argued that "the CAAP has to be stopped at this point and a new beginning must be made or this program is doomed."[35] He suggested an alternative plan that he believed was better suited to the mission of the War on Poverty. He proposed that the executive committee the mayor had appointed be "un-appointed" and that the CAAP board elect a new executive committee. Furthermore, he argued that the forty-member CAAP board should be expanded to fifty and that "existing neighborhood associations, church alliances and other organizations in the poverty areas" nominate at least twenty-one of these members.[36] Newton believed strongly that "the poor must have a majority vote on the CAAP board if the program is to succeed."[37]

Newton's plan differed markedly from the mayor's. Most importantly, Newton's proposals—based on the premise that the poor should have a voice—would have empowered neighborhood residents themselves. Newton insisted that "representatives of the poverty areas must be genuine representatives. The concept of a committee picking acceptable poverty area people for the board must be rejected." He charged that "once a person is 'picked' in this manner he loses the trust of his neighbors. He is seen as a pawn in the hands of 'the people uptown.'"[38] Frank Meech, Barton's assistant, retorted that the "critics don't understand why CAAP was created," and that "persons directly representing poverty interests will be appointed at a later date."[39]

When it became clear that Barton was unwilling to alter the structure of CAAP, Newton decided to leave Indianapolis to work for the War on Poverty in the state of Kentucky. But because he had assumed such a visible profile through his criticisms of the mayor, the *Indianapolis Times* featured Newton's departure in a front-page story. Newton described how he had been told that poor people were not allowed on the executive committee of CAAP because "they [the political elites] say we don't represent anyone." Responding to the fact that African Americans in particular were not adequately represented, he complained that the city's elite have always "selected acceptable Negro leaders, rather than accepted the real Negro leadership." He urged Indianapolis residents, if they hoped to change this practice, to follow men like Reverend Andrew J. Brown, a "real leader—a man whose advice should be sought."[40] Warning that the road ahead would be difficult, Newton declared, "Indianapolis has never understood the democratic form of government. Its leaders only listen to established groups. It eventually forces us (poor people) to organize also."[41] Newton left Indianapolis rather than continue his fight to democratize the CAAP in large part because he believed it was a battle with little chance for victory.

Although his most vociferous critic had left town, Barton could not ignore the chorus of criticism that had emerged in April 1965. In fact, shortly after Newton's departure, Barton tried in May to mollify dissent when he announced plans to enlarge the executive committee from eleven to thirteen members "to give broader representation to poverty groups and major educational and religious groups."[42] The mayor even offered seats on the forty-member board to erstwhile critics, including a member of the Christian Inner City Association. His concessions, however, backfired.

A Community Divided

If heated debates had been conducted between those on the CAAP board and those left out, Barton now unwittingly ensured that conflict would be played out within the new board, as new members pushed for programs that the conservative board had resisted. Between the summer of 1965, when Barton democratized the board, and the fall of 1968, when conservative board members once again gained complete control, the board remained divided. On one side stood the city's political and civic elite, who continued to dominate the board and try to fit the War on Poverty into the traditional social welfare system. On the other side were African Americans and white sympathizers, many of whom were ministers, who understood their involvement in the CAAP board as a way to empower poor African Americans. The inner workings of the board and its members' relations to specific programs illuminate how the War on Poverty actually worked within the urban context. Not all War on Poverty programs generated conflict within the CAAP board. For example, all board members supported Head Start and Manpower. However, the conservative members opposed offering lunches through Head Start because food assistance "do[es] not belong in an 'educational program.' "[43] Board consensus withered when it came to the neighborhood centers and the Legal Services Organization (LSO). Liberal board members who supported these programs appreciated how they operated outside of the reach of traditional social welfare providers and were run instead by individuals who hoped to bring greater power to disadvantaged communities. In contrast, conservatives on the board considered these programs an intrusion upon local social welfare practices.

For better or worse, both conservatives and liberals recognized neighborhood centers as a central component of the War on Poverty. Liberals in the Johnson administration hoped the community action agencies and the neighborhood centers funded by the Community Action Program would provide basic services—employment training and day nurseries—*and* a place where the poor could begin "'shaking the system' and forcing change on reluctant school administrators, welfare and employment service officials, and even settlement houses and Community Chest leaders."[44] In contrast to traditional social settlement houses of the early twentieth century, where upper and middle class citizens "served" the poor, the neighborhood centers were to be run by and for the poor themselves.

The Martindale Area Citizens Service (MACS), the largest of Indianapolis's seven neighborhood centers, provides an excellent example of the practices of neighborhood centers and the conflicts they generated among the board members and within the larger society. Martindale, one of the city's poorest neighborhoods, was more than 95 percent black. Residents' average income in 1960 was $3,633, 40 percent lower than the citywide average. Martindale's unemployment rate was double the city's average, and 57 percent of the housing was rated as dilapidated or deteriorated.[45] The Edna Martin Center and a few religious congregations were the only institutions providing basic social services. The most active of these congregations was St. Rita's, led by Father Bernard Strange, who recognized that voluntary and traditional efforts to deal with poverty were doomed. Strange joined forces with Faye Williams, one of his parishioners, to head up MACS, and he offered St. Rita's to house MACS's activities. They made clear, however, that they did not want MACS to operate like a traditional social settlement house, where the wealthy provided for the needy under a cloak of *noblesse oblige*. Instead, they invited the poor to speak for themselves and to address the problems they themselves had identified. MACS employed residents to canvass their neighborhood, and in these house-to-house visits, the residents explained "what MACS and the War on Poverty were all about [and asked] what improvements or changes the people wanted to see." Most important, they described MACS as a center "promoting neighborhood organization, decentralization of city services and humanizing of city government."[46]

Within months of receiving its first federal funds in the summer of 1965, MACS developed into a full-fledged neighborhood center, employing more than forty neighborhood residents. Father Strange's rallying cry, "We live in a slum and we're tired of it," encapsulated the frustrations of the neighborhood's residents, and many of them flocked to MACS.[47] Working women used the day nurseries while their older children attended Head Start classes. Neighborhood residents of all ages received much-needed medical care and legal advice. Others engaged in more explicitly political activities, pressuring city government to provide more money for low-cost housing and organizing public assistance recipients to demand respectful treatment and greater funding from public welfare authorities. Finally, the men and women at MACS encouraged neighborhood residents to register to vote, encouraging political participation.

Notwithstanding MACS's success, opposition to it grew strong, especially among conservative CAAP board members who feared MACS's political power. As one federal official put it, the conservatives in Indianapolis "object to the funding of the Martindale Area Project as use of tax funds for political action."[48] Once conservative board members realized that the neighborhood centers could be used to promote political activity, they grossly underfunded the city's other six neighborhood centers and abandoned plans to establish an additional three centers. Board member William Clark, an African American clergyman who acted as the official liaison between the CAAP board and the neighborhood centers, bore much of the heat because he had gained a reputation for encouraging greater participation of the poor in the design and administration of neighborhood centers.

The strongest opposition to MACS and other neighborhood centers came from Indianapolis's traditional social welfare providers, many of whom gained seats on the CAAP board in order to curb its influence. For example, when Faye Williams and Father Strange proposed that MACS host a "health coordinator," Dr. Henry G. Nester, city-county health director and CAAP board member, stated flatly that he "did not believe in it." Health services, he argued, should "go through existing agencies" and "the appointment of a health educator there [at MACS] would simply duplicate work being done now by the County Health Department." Nester clearly feared loss of control over the services provided. He responded caustically when, over his objections, the CAAP board approved the health coordinator. "What are we going to do? Have another health department?" Referring to CAAP's original plan for ten neighborhood centers, Nester wondered, "Does this mean we'll have ten health departments in the city?"[49]

Nester was not alone in his resistance to neighborhood centers. William Stanton, director of the Marion County Department of

Public Welfare, was a particularly vocal critic of the neighborhood centers and he, like Nester, sat on the CAAP board. On more than one occasion, Stanton questioned why it was necessary to create these new neighborhood centers and suggested that the War on Poverty would be more successful if CAAP channeled federal funds through pre-existing centralized agencies such as the public welfare department. He often complained that "CAAP has spent too much time organizing people to be ultra-critical, and not in a constructive sense."[50] What Stanton failed to realize, or maybe understood too well, was that the more progressive federal authorities had supported the neighborhood centers precisely because they did not want traditional social welfare agencies, which were believed to be part of the problem, administering War on Poverty programs. When officials from the federal Office of Economic Opportunity released funds for Indianapolis's neighborhood centers in the spring of 1966, they stated explicitly that the main activity of these centers should be to "mobilize the people of the designated neighborhoods for direct action to secure an equitable distribution of power, including seeking a 'Fair Deal' in housing."[51]

One of the more vocal and politically active groups in Indianapolis was the Welfare Rights Organization (WRO), which Faye Williams helped organize at MACS. Across the nation women organized WROs that protested the punitive attitudes of public welfare workers and the low levels of support welfare recipients received.[52] The WROs focused considerable attention on the "suitable home" clauses, which allowed welfare workers to deny public assistance to women deemed morally unfit and gave them the power to make "midnight" raids on the homes of women receiving public assistance. During these raids, social workers wanted to make sure that no men, either the fathers of the children or unrelated men, were present. In Indianapolis, women who joined the WRO had good reason to be upset. Ever since the passage in 1935 of the federal New Deal program Aid to Dependent Children (ADC) (later renamed Aid to Families with Dependent Children), Indiana had ranked near the bottom in the number of women receiving aid. In 1958, Indiana provided aid to only half the number of women as the national average, and the amount each mother received was also considerably less than the national average.⁵³ Indiana ranked forty-sixth out of all states when measured in terms of the number of women receiving assistance and forty-eighth when measured in terms of the amount of assistance per inhabitant.

Social workers employed by the state were required to abide by guidelines established by policy makers who were intent on limiting if not dismantling this federal program. One of the first assaults on public assistance occurred in 1943 when the Indiana state legislature passed a resolution for a study to be conducted of the Indiana Department of Public Welfare by a Welfare Investigation Committee. The committee—made up of three state senators and three representatives—listed in their final report the grievances Indiana politicians had of the ADC program. The committee complained that "the worthiness of the individual" wasn't a bigger factor in determining who received aid. "We consider it to be both dangerous and unsound to attempt, much less actually accomplish, an irrevocable shift from old-fashioned concepts of thrift, industry, and self-help to any so called modern concept of need regardless of anything else as a basis for public assistance." Public assistance had gone awry, the committee claimed, because of the "dictatorial instructions received from the [federal] Social Security Board."⁵⁴

Criticism of ADC fed into and accentuated the strong anti–federal government sentiment that had always been a part of Indiana political culture. The Welfare Investigation Committee members, however, moved beyond abstract sentiments and proposed concrete solutions. The committee wanted to strengthen the authority of local county welfare departments to "free them from the domination which now exists." In a test of will against federal power, the committee suggested that all unwed mothers who apply for aid should automatically be sent to the court and that their children be made wards of the court. The court, then, rather than the Department of Public Welfare, would have the power to decide both whether the women should retain custody of their children and whether or not they were deserving of public support. This proposal set a precedent for the legislature to attempt to use local judicial powers to shape public assistance.⁵⁵

The climate in Indianapolis became even more hostile for single mothers in the 1960s and 1970s when public authorities, including William Stanton, head of the Marion County Department of Public Welfare, helped mobilize a full-fledged campaign against public assistance recipients. The key to this campaign was the racialization of welfare.

When it was first instituted in 1935, white widowed women made up the majority of ADC recipients. Many states routinely refused aid to African American women, even the most desperate. This practice reflected the assumption that white children were best cared for by full-time mothers and that only white widowed women were deserving of public support.[56] In the 1950s, however, African American women finally began to receive the public aid to which they were entitled. As the black unwed mother became the face of welfare itself, opposition to it mounted.

In Indianapolis, Stanton and other opponents of public assistance were aided by the local press, which in the early 1960s focused considerable attention on African American welfare recipients, whom they described as "lazy and immoral."[57] In one article, the *Indianapolis Times* highlighted an African American woman who had six children by six different fathers and who "knew no moral law, only the law of the street."[58] These racialized images entered popular consciousness and provided Stanton with an opportunity to revamp Indiana's public welfare system.

Stanton followed the lead of welfare officials in states like Louisiana when he attempted to cut off from public assistance all women who bore additional children while receiving ADC. Similarly, it was the racialization of welfare that moved Stanton to join forces with Circuit Judge John L. Nisbeck, who headed an effort to "permit authorities to place for adoption the children of any women who have more than three out of wedlock children."[59] In defense of the measure, Stanton described how there were one hundred women in Indianapolis receiving ADC who had had three or more illegitimate children, stating with great indignation, "ninety-eight of the one hundred are Negro women."[60] Recognizing that it would be impossible to find adoptive homes for so many African American children if the measure passed, Nisbeck responded, "They will be better off being raised in an orphans' home."[61] Even though the Indiana General Assembly refused to pass the bill, there was a widespread belief in the larger society that through ADC, the government offered "public support of immorality."[62] Growing opposition to welfare also made it possible for Stanton to propose a law requiring the sterilization of any woman with two or more children who, while receiving public support, became pregnant again and requested additional support.[63] Neither Stanton nor Nisbeck had qualms about denying poor women the basic civil right to raise their own children, a right that the middle class took for granted.

Indianapolis's WROs faced formidable obstacles because of the long history of opposition to public assistance. However, the WROs nonetheless found support from the CICA and religious organizations frustrated with the city's welfare agencies and committed to neighborhood centers and the WRO as a means to empower women. For example, Catholic Social Services looked with pride upon the active role Catholics played in MACS. Catholic Social Services complained that the Township Trustee system, which routinely failed to authorize federal food stamps for the eligible poor, was "an antiquated way to provide general assistance" and was actually "a way of giving as little as possible." The leaders of Catholic Social Services went even further, contending that the state of Indiana as a whole evinced a "punitive attitude toward welfare."[64] For Catholics committed to the idea that all children needed the care and oversight of their mothers, such attitudes threatened the sanctity of the family and the most basic rights of both women and children.

Organizations like the WRO drew the ire of many within the city beyond the conservative board members of CAAP and public welfare administrators. In a highly polemical editorial entitled "Self-Help Ignored," Ross Hermann, a writer for the *Indianapolis News,* criticized MACS for its "emphasis on organization and collective action." He argued that the activities of the WRO proved that MACS was "firmly in the hands of inspired amateurs, political activists, and worse."[65] Most revealing, Hermann felt that the poor would be better off not by challenging the system, but by focusing on "self-help." Like other Indianapolis conservatives, Hermann resisted the federal mandate for maximum feasible participation of the poor in the War on Poverty and instead expected federal support to adapt itself to the city's traditional social welfare system, one in which there was little discussion of civil or social rights.

Like Hermann, Flanner House executive director Cleo Blackburne juxtaposed maximum feasible participation of the poor against America's tradition of "self-help." Blackburne resented neighborhood centers and charged they had stolen social workers from private social agencies and driven up wages. He wanted more emphasis placed on "self-help" projects like the maid training program offered at Flanner House. Blackburne's opposition to Faye Williams and the WRO was so strong that he never even mentioned Williams's collaborative work with the Marion County Department of Public Welfare. But in the spring of 1967, Williams had headed up a pilot project to train welfare recipients as nurses' aides. The public welfare department paid these women benefits and MACS provided their training.[66] While Williams made significant overtures to the welfare department, she nonetheless defended her right to criticize its abuses and, as a result, found herself labeled a "militant."[67]

The neighborhood centers and the WRO generated heat, but they were not alone among War on Poverty programs. Conservatives also attacked the Legal Services Organization (LSO), which provided legal representation to poor people in civil matters. Fearing the empowerment of the poor, Carl Dortch, executive vice president of the Indianapolis Chamber of Commerce and CAAP board member, voted against the LSO, claiming the "beneficiaries will be the lawyers not the poor."[68] Other opponents insisted that the program would "dry up the sources for many practicing attorneys."[69]

The LSO's sheer volume of work for the poor revealed how the poor had been denied access to adequate legal counsel, a matter LSO opponents ignored. In less than two years, LSO's eleven attorneys handled more than 9,000 cases, the vast majority of which they won. Their clients, who earned less than $3,000 a year to qualify for assistance, sought help with a variety of matters, from challenging unfair tenant evictions to forcing ex-husbands to pay child support.

LSO lawyers and clients insisted that access to legal counsel cut to the heart of all civil and social rights. Without such access, other basic rights were also threatened. Many conservatives, however, vigorously opposed the LSO. Circuit Judge John L. Nisbeck warned the Indianapolis Bar Association that oversaw the LSO that "the Bar Association is either going to be entirely out of business or else be on the Federal payroll, financed by the tax-payer and drawing salaries from OEO."[70] In the spring of 1968, Nisbeck banned the eleven lawyers at the LSO from his circuit county court. Explaining his actions, he claimed that LSO attorneys had missed court dates. In response to the ban, George Sawyer, the head of the LSO, informed a reporter that "80% of the poor are Negroes and, by God, he [Nisbeck] is doing more damage to the Negro in Indianapolis than anyone else." To reassure the black population that the LSO would not desert them, Sawyer declared, "We are charged with insuring justice to the poor people. No one will hinder or stop this process."[71] To the larger community Sawyer claimed that what really bothered Nisbeck was that "federal funds [are] used to operate LSO."[72]

Judge Nisbeck, in order to mobilize support, characterized the War on Poverty and the LSO as a form of federal domination. Prior to the mid-1960s, Indianapolis had accepted very few federal dollars, with the exception of federal money for Social Security programs. To justify this practice, politicians had extolled the virtues of Hoosier independence and played upon fears that federal money would lead to "federal control." Several counties had refused to participate in the War on Poverty because, as one Boone County official put it, they did not want to deal with "federal regulations with a lot of strings attached."[73] An official in Hancock County explained that federal funds were unnecessary because "it is wealthy enough to 'take care of its own.' "[74] Nisbeck took advantage of these pervasive sentiments. However, Sawyer responded to Nisbeck's offensive against the LSO: "It should be made crystal clear LSO is a locally controlled Indiana corporation. Its board of directors is composed of a majority of lawyers who are chosen by the Bar Association, the NAACP, and lawyers representing poor people."[75] Critics of the War on Poverty in Indianapolis complained that it was a "federal" program under federal control. While the issue of local control was certainly important, this rhetoric masked fears about the empowerment of poor people. In fact, the War on Poverty actually provided more local control than most federally funded programs, but "local" control had multiple meanings. For some it implied grass-roots efforts, but for Indianapolis's traditional elite, local control meant elite domination, and the War on Poverty's demand for the maximum feasible participation of the poor represented an unwelcome intrusion into local political practices.

Without Victory

Conflicts over the neighborhood centers and the LSO demonstrated how Mayor Barton's attempt to generate community support for CAAP by democratizing its board had failed. Between 1965 and 1968, conservative and liberal board members repeatedly divided over what programs to support. These divisions became especially stark in the fall of 1967 when the conservatives attempted to gain complete control of the board. In response, the African American clergy who led the liberal faction called on the federal government to intervene.

Between 1965 and 1967, those board members who supported the independent actions of the neighborhood centers, or who backed the LSO, found themselves under attack. Reverend William Clark, assistant executive director of CAAP neighborhood centers, provoked criticism for encouraging the poor to take an active role in the activities at the centers. Reverend Mozell Sanders, vice president of the CAAP board, elicited anger from his conservative colleagues because he was "prominent in [the Baptist Ministers' Alliance] Commission's attacks on the Board."[76]

Clark and Sanders found themselves increasingly isolated from the board. Sanders, who "often finds himself at odds with the Board over personnel practices and the handling of the neighborhood services division," complained that his colleagues referred to him as a "troublemaker" and that he was "often not informed of meetings when important decisions are to be made."[77] One conservative board member, when questioned about Sanders, claimed that Sanders and the Baptist Ministers' Alliance "are acting in a way quite reminiscent of another pressure group, Homes Before Highways Inc.," an organization that had protested the destruction of poor, largely black, neighborhoods to make way for a new highway.[78]

The tension between the two factions of CAAP degenerated when Clark was fired from his position at CAAP in the fall of 1967. The CAAP board claimed Clark had failed to report adequately on the activities of the neighborhood centers and had released "unauthorized information to the news media." His supporters countered that Clark was fired because he was "too strong an advocate for the poor."[79]

As a result of Clark's departure, CAAP found itself the target of heated criticism. African American clergy again led the protest. The Indianapolis Baptist Foresight Alliance and the Baptist Alliance Commission met with Mrs. Helen McCalumet, CAAP board president, to protest Clark's dismissal. They called for his reinstatement and insisted that the CAAP board needed to be reconfigured to give control to "a group of dedicated and competent persons representing the total community."[80] The ministers argued that poor people must run their own neighborhood centers and that they required more money. Clearly the African American community found Barton's democratization of the board a shallow gesture that had failed to lead the poor into the active role over War on Poverty programs.

To compel concessions from local authorities, the clergy campaigned to attract national attention. The ministers were eager to demonstrate that they truly represented Indianapolis's poor black population and that federal OEO authorities should embrace their vision of CAAP. Reverend B. T. Almon, president of the Foresight Alliance, told McCalumet that the one hundred churches in his neighborhood were so incensed by the CAAP board that they wanted the federal OEO to cut off funds until the program was democratized.[81] Following the lead of national religious organizations such as the Interreligious Committee Against Poverty, which testified before the U.S. Congress in support of higher allocations for the War on Poverty, Indianapolis's ministerial associations sent telegrams outlining CAAP abuses to directors of the OEO, Representative Andrew Jacobs, Jr., and Senator Birch Bayh. The ministers alleged "systematic discrimination against employees who are concerned about the mission and function of the CAAP program and who demonstrate creativity and aggressiveness in performing their duties." The ministers even accused CAAP of discrimination against forward-looking employees in "a planned effort on the part of the administration to sabotage the program."[82] Critics in Indianapolis charged that Mayor Barton, after three years of overseeing the CAAP board, saw CAAP as a political liability and was trying to distance himself from it or undermine it. In contrast, African American clergy, disillusioned with CAAP, claimed that "what was thought to be a 'War on poverty' has become a War on people" in which "political deals, trickery, and duplicity have been used against the poor people of the community."[83] Even the head of the Church Federation, Reverend Benjamin Davis, joined the chorus of criticism. Davis charged CAAP with "flagrant irresponsibility in the handing of the local poverty program." Very few African Americans were involved in administrative positions and, Davis continued, "the Negro community is no longer willing to accept or tolerate black tokenism."[84]

Just two months after the African American ministers had gone public with their concerns, the OEO decided to investigate. Federal officials interviewed CAAP members, reviewed CAAP files and programs, and vindicated the clergy. The officials found that CAAP had failed to provide adequate representation for the poor on the board. In addition, the authorities discovered that "staff members who were 'fired' with charges of incompetence, insubordination, or violation of basic conditions of employment really were dismissed for other reasons" and that CAAP "has not been a model of the democratic process." Equally damning, the investigators discerned among board members "static or confused attitudes." In particular they found that some members "express concern with the need to deal with the 'basic causes of poverty' while not challenging those forces whose welfare requires continuation of those basic causes."[85] Put clearly, board members responsible for administering the War on Poverty helped to create the causes of poverty. The OEO froze all War on Poverty funds in Indianapolis until a number of conditions were met. The OEO insisted upon "evidence of adequate community support which demonstrates a cross section of the community" and "evidence that target area residents were involved in the preparation and planning of the refunding applications."[86] In addition, investigators suggested that CAAP board meetings be held somewhere other than the city-county building. The investigators claimed, "while the location is generally convenient, it is also close to the political 'powers that be' and far from the neighborhoods and people to which the program is directed."[87]

Vindicated by the federal investigation, the Baptist Ministers' Alliance, which included Reverend Brown, took aggressive steps to certify that CAAP met the federal government's conditions. They raised $500 to hire an "outsider" to help CAAP in its reorganization, a significant symbolic act that communicated the African American clergy's investment in the War on Poverty. They hired Dr. John T. Liell, a sociologist from Indiana University, who they hoped could plan "an effective program with functional participation by the poor at all levels of the program."[88] Thanks in part to the actions of the Baptist Ministers' Alliance, Indianapolis's CAAP once again began to receive federal money.

If it appeared that African Americans would finally have a greater impact on Indianapolis's War on Poverty, their hopes were soon dashed. In August 1968 Helen McCalumet, president of the board, announced the men and women who had been chosen by CAAP's nominating committee to stand for election to the board. To the astonishment of the African American clergy, who had financed Liell's appointment, neither the Baptist Ministers' Alliance's candidate, Reverend J. R. Bradley, pastor of First Baptist Church of North Indianapolis, nor the SCLC's candidate, civil rights activist Reverend Andrew J. Brown, were chosen to stand for election. Nominations for the elections had been selected by powerful civic organizations, such as the Chamber of Commerce, as tradition had dictated. Even more shocking to the African American community, Reverend Mozell Sanders was overlooked for the presidency of

CAAP in favor of John W. Walls. Sanders had experience working among the poor and with CAAP. Walls, later that year, became administrative assistant to Republican Richard Lugar, who won the 1968 mayoral race. Reverend Andrew J. Brown quipped sarcastically, "We would hate to think that the nominating committee reflects the feelings of the power structure that Reverend Sanders is too militant and outspoken as a defender of the poor."[89]

At first glance it seems surprising that the African American clergy were excluded from the CAAP board. They had worked so hard to democratize CAAP and to support it financially when the federal government had cut its funds. But when placed within the context of other events taking place in 1968, it makes sense. Resistance to the War on Poverty among conservatives was mounting in Indianapolis and across the nation. While CAAP had received more than three million dollars in 1968, two years later the appropriation fell to less than one and a half million.[90] Nationally, appropriations also fell. Finally, the election of Richard Nixon to the presidency put the nails in the coffin of the War on Poverty, while Lugar's Indianapolis mayoralty ensured that CAAP would look very different. Not long into Lugar's term, everyone understood that "many of the neighborhood centers will be given a different emphasis or phased out." More specifically, "if the neighborhood centers are maintained, their primary role would be channeling the poor to traditional social service agencies in the community rather than providing those services themselves or acting as a voice for the poor."[91] Changes at MACS bore this prediction out. In November 1968 the center lost its independence and was incorporated into the Model City program under direct control of the mayor's office.[92] While CAAP survived as an administrative body, it no longer mobilized residents to demand an equitable distribution of power.

The political winds blew dramatically in the fall of 1968. Citizens who had hoped that the War on Poverty would provide an opportunity to expand citizenship rights and gain a place for the less advantaged in Indianapolis's formal decision making circles were disappointed. Frustrations ran high. Donald Schmidlin, a white Catholic priest, lamented that "CAAP can't get to the causes of poverty because this country is not ready to admit what those causes are. And the chief cause is that our economic system does not help the poor." More caustically, he asserted, "NOBODY in Indianapolis is really concerned about poverty. They have regarded CAAP as a joke from the beginning. The establishment has nothing to gain by eradicating poverty."[93] In 1969 the *Indianapolis News* captured the irony of the War on Poverty. "The reason CAAP has not received as much local support as it might have, is that in fulfilling one of its roles of providing a voice for the poor, it wound up confronting institutions such as the city government, schools, and other agencies. While this may have been a legitimate role for CAAP, it presents some political problems, namely in that CAAP winds up appearing to bite the hand that should feed it."[94] With Republican Richard Lugar in the mayor's office, CAAP abandoned the goals that the clergy had supported. Liell summed up this new direction best in 1970 when he stated, "CAAP is fighting to preserve the system. Our goals are basically conservative. We must show that the system can work, and that all can share in our prosperity."[95]

The conflicts surrounding the War on Poverty in Indianapolis make clear that the home front had never been united. The *Indianapolis Star* described how "those of a conservative bent complain that the anti-poverty program is poorly organized and pads the pockets of street gang leaders and fundamentalist preachers."[96] These conservatives felt that the War on Poverty had been ill conceived and that the money would have been better spent if directed to traditional welfare agencies. In contrast, the CICA and the black ministerial associations expressed disappointment that they never acquired power to use the War on Poverty to challenge racial and class inequalities. Federal authorities familiar with Indianapolis agreed with the clergy when they reported that CAAP "fails to be democratic."[97]

The War on Poverty, however, did not entirely fail to empower the poor. Many African American clergy who protested elite co-optation of the War on Poverty won a political hearing. In the years and decades after the War on Poverty, they would continue to be heard and provide a focal point for the black community. Perhaps most important, the War on Poverty unveiled the interconnections between race and economics and shed light on questions about the nature of citizenship and democracy. Without denying that the vote was the most essential right of citizenship, supporters of the War on Poverty asked fundamental questions about social and civil rights. They raised critical issues about whether or not poor people who lacked access to adequate housing or legal representation truly were among America's fully entitled citizens.

IV

"BEYOND RELIGIOUS BOUNDARIES": URBAN MINISTRY AND SOCIAL ORDER

Reflecting on the rise of urban ministries in Indianapolis during the 1960s and early 1970s, a reporter for the *Indianapolis News* observed, "There was a time when a church's charity work was done across town, in a place few of the congregations ever saw. Those times are gone now, at least for many of the proud old churches whose neighborhoods, once the most exclusive in the city, gradually gave way to inner city decay." This was the case for Trinity Episcopal at 3243 Meridian Street, where Reverend Lynch confirmed, "Churches have always helped those in need. It's just that now, if we're talking about mission work, there's work to be done right under our noses."[1]

Before the 1960s, most Indianapolis congregations concentrated on serving the spiritual and social needs of their own members. This changed in the 1960s as religious leaders and laity confronted intense racial, social, and economic changes occurring in their own churches' neighborhoods. If the War on Poverty pushed African American and politically engaged white clergy to consider the role of religious institutions in the city, most Catholic and mainline Protestant churches failed to see the relevance of the federal initiative for their churches. However, massive urban demographic transformations, such as deindustrialization and white flight, compelled them to rethink their urban responsibilities.

Like other Midwestern and eastern industrial cities in the 1950s and 1960s, Indianapolis witnessed dramatic migration of white residents to the suburbs. Although Indianapolis did not suffer from as severe depopulation and deindustrialization as Chicago and Detroit, its middle-class whites were nonetheless drawn to the suburbs, made accessible to the downtown workforce by highway construction. The poor and nonwhite remained in the city and were not welcome in the suburbs.

The impact of "white flight" on urban housing prices and business has been well documented.[2] Churches also felt the effects. In the 1950s and 1960s, in Indianapolis and in other urban centers, approximately one-third of all congregations closed or moved.[3] In contrast to previous decades, in the 1960s, large, wealthy, white mainline churches were overrepresented among relocated congregations.[4] Middle-class white churches generally followed congregants who moved to the suburbs, creating what one reporter dubbed a "honeymoon in suburban communities."[5] The immediate postwar period recorded some of the highest levels of church attendance and church building in American history. In Indianapolis, denominational planning commissions helped organize this new growth.[6]

Notwithstanding religious exuberance in the suburbs, a minority of white, middle-class Protestant congregations chose to remain in the city and redefine their identity and mission. Although historians know that urban Catholic parishes necessarily remained anchored to urban space because their canonical definition required them to minister to all residents in their neighborhood, we know less about Protestant congregations who self-consciously remained and remade their identity.[7] In Indianapolis, Protestant urban clergy and congregants came to understand their churches as "neighborhood" institutions with an obligation to respond to the social needs of their neighbors, regardless of whether nearby residents were congregational members. Urban congregations established a broad range of programs, from day care centers to employment training, as they committed themselves to their neighborhoods and developed a territorial-based vision of ministry. As Superintendent Gerald Clapsaddle of the Indianapolis district of the Methodist Church explained, "Protestant clergy are working to develop a parish type of ministry in the inner city."[8]

As urban congregations committed themselves to their neighborhoods, some churches also took on urban issues through interdenominational housing nonprofits, ecumenical pastoral groups, and participation in the War on Poverty and neighborhood associations. Urban congregations were sensitive to the impact of policy makers, who reflected Indianapolis's conservative political culture, and encouraged private institutions such as churches to address social problems in neighborhoods.

In addition, religious and secular nonprofits tapped resources that became available when the federal government began to channel money to the private sector in the late 1960s. The dismemberment of War on Poverty programs did not curtail the federal government's outreach to nonprofit organizations, as some had expected. In fact, the federal government in the late 1960s relied more heavily upon nonprofits.[9] In Indianapolis, the number of religiously affiliated organizations receiving public funds increased significantly, filling them with dreamy expectations that they could solve urban social problems. Although few clergy could have predicted how difficult their missions would be and how quickly enthusiasm would dissipate among both religious laity and public authorities, congregations took up their urban missions armed with the confidence that they had a special role to play in revitalizing the city.

The Constructed City

In the early 1960s, the Indianapolis Community Service Council (CSC), later renamed the United Way, began to conduct surveys of the city. CSC planners followed the lead of their national parent organization, which had expanded its focus from establishing social work practices and standards to research and analysis to solve social, economic, and racial problems. With federal census demographic and spatial data and information gathered locally, the Indianapolis CSC confirmed the obvious: whites fled the city as blacks moved into neighborhoods previously closed to them. In addition, the city as a whole became much poorer.

According to historian Etan Diamond, the most dramatic changes occurred in the Mapleton–Fall Creek area on the northeast side, where neighborhoods that in 1950 were more than 80 percent white turned 79 percent black by 1970. Elsewhere, even though the racial turnover was less dramatic, it was significant. Near-westside neighborhoods saw the number of African Americans rise from 13.6 percent to 31.9 percent in the same years. In the Martindale-Brightwood neighborhood, evenly divided between whites and blacks in 1950 (blacks lived in the Martindale section and whites in Brightwood), whites fled en masse. By 1970 more than half of the whites had left, and by 1990 the area would become 95 percent black. Center Township, the old city limits of Indianapolis, witnessed an increase of black residents from 30 percent in 1940 to 70 percent in 1970. As the African American population increased, so too did poverty and unemployment levels.[10] Charting these demographic changes and examining each region of the city separately with a profile of residents and social resources available to those residents, the CSC surveys helped set Indianapolis's policy agenda.

In the 1940s and 1950s, urban policy makers and planners had concentrated on metropolitan and regional development, often ignoring differences among neighborhoods. In the 1960s, by contrast, planners and civic leaders believed city institutions—private and public, secular and religious—needed a firm understanding of neighborhoods and the concerns of urban residents in order to effectively serve the poor nonwhite population. It was no longer acceptable to conduct urban planning that did not take into account the neighborhood as a social and economic unit. Indianapolis was not unique. As historian Patricia Melvin explains, throughout the nation the "neighborhood" became the "staging ground for solutions to contemporary problems."[11] This was true of the War on Poverty as well as of the federal and local initiatives that followed it.

Even though urban planners paid greater heed to neighborhood development, specific initiatives reflected the unique political cultures of each city. Thus, Indianapolis civic leaders brought their conservative traditions to bear when they turned their attention to urban neighborhoods. Although conservatives had resisted War on Poverty neighborhood initiatives as a federal intrusion, they did not reject neighborhood development per se. Instead, Indianapolis civic leaders wed their new neighborhood awareness to their belief that social problems were primarily the responsibility of private citizens and institutions, not public authorities.

The CSC, a principal agent responsible for urban social welfare policy, mobilized existing institutions to address urban problems. It looked to organizations with, or the potential to develop, neighborhood roots. It encouraged settlement houses that had become disconnected from their neighborhoods to get more involved and allow local residents to help shape settlement agendas. Significantly, the CSC argued that churches should be "of interest to general social and community planning because of the potential offered by them for wider community service."[12]

Indianapolis's elite looked to congregations because they were the most numerous and geographically dispersed private institutions, grounded in neighborhoods in need of assistance. However, in 1961 the CSC focused on the *potential* of congregations because most congregations had neither attended to nor studied their neighborhoods. Congregations had as their primary mission spiritual fellowship, and many restricted social and recreational programs to members.[13] So long as membership remained stable, most congregations remained oblivious to the needs of their neighborhoods or the role of their churches for the entire city.

Urban Ministries

It is one thing for a church to be located in a city and another thing altogether for it to identify itself as an urban institution. In fact, most congregations in urban areas did not describe themselves as "urban" before 1960. The birth of "urban ministry" as a special type of ministry in the 1960s signaled a rethinking of religion's role in the city and society. National denominational leaders encouraged this process in order to make their resources responsive and relevant to white flight and high-profile urban racial and class inequalities. Unwilling to abandon America's inner cities, they set out to "understand" urban America and respond appropriately to its residents. New denominational "urban departments" led the way.

They published journals, sponsored conferences where religious leaders debated their responsibilities to the nation's cities, and discussed how to address poverty, housing needs, racial discrimination, and police brutality.[14] Although some denominations, such as the United Methodist Church and the Presbyterian Church U.S.A., were more active than others, most began in one way or another to reconsider religion's role in the city, and many joined ecumenical efforts in their quest to become more relevant to urban life.

In Indianapolis the Church Federation was decisive to the development of urban ministries. Established in 1912, the Federation, with links to the National Conference of Churches, was the voice of mainline Protestantism. Before the 1960s the key "public" issues it focused on were blue laws and prayer in public school. In the 1960s the Federation's concerns shifted in response to larger cultural and social changes. In 1963 the Church Federation conducted a study to "discover how the churches working together can form a more effective ecumenical force in the city." In response to that study, the Federation established an "Inner City Task Force."[15] The Inner City Task Force articulated a vision of urban ministry that challenged dearly held beliefs about urban churches. The Federation began with the premise that "our denominational leaders and church laity have got to learn that the Inner City cannot be reached by the traditional evangelistic approach" and that the church must "not assume it will build up self supporting congregations or measure its success by the number of people it gets into the congregation."[16]

Because both evangelical and mainline Protestant churches, according to the Church Federation, had generally defined their relationship to the city in evangelistic terms, such a proposition looked threatening. However, rejecting traditional evangelical methods and goals was only one step toward an effective urban ministry. The Federation also demanded that churches "recognize that any effective Inner City Ministry must involve the people themselves in the decision making process." Although many members of the Federation had reservations about the War on Poverty, the idea that the poor could no longer be merely "served," but must be listened to, was becoming mainstream. The Federation encouraged its member churches to "convers[e] with them [the people] at their point of interests and needs" and to focus on a wide range of issues, such as housing, voting, poverty, and welfare assistance.[17]

Not all Federation congregations embraced the new understanding of urban ministry, nor were they all willing to abandon traditional evangelical methods. Many thought the Federation should continue to focus on issues of public morality and avoid the example set by the National Council of Churches, which in the 1960s became increasingly political. Under the leadership of men like Laurence Hosie and Robert Koenig, however, the Federation refused to abandon its new course. Koenig, a minister in the Evangelical United Brethren Church, had sat on the Federation's board and led its evangelistic committee in the 1950s.[18] He also served on the Community Action Against Poverty board from 1968 to 1971.[19] Koenig believed that the Federation must "reinterpret for all our churches their responsibility for the Inner City."[20] Federation leaders like Koenig encouraged churches to "study the city" and become familiar with its "unmet needs."[21] Recognizing that churches would have to work alongside other urban institutions, the Federation nudged clergy to make contact with both "private and public social welfare agencies."[22] To facilitate these relationships, the Federation created programs like EXPOsure that brought clergy on "walking tours of the inner city." During the tours, the Federation introduced clergy to important officials at the Township Trustee Office, the Juvenile Court, Community Action Against Poverty, the Marion County Department of Public Welfare, and the Legal Services Organization.[23] The Federation also fostered the training of urban pastors and was glad to report in 1967 that both the Methodists and Presbyterians had plans in place to employ "full-time metropolitan ministers."[24]

Even as the Church Federation contemplated how to encourage ecumenical efforts and teach churches about their responsibility for the city, individual congregations began their own urban ministries. Although these ministries varied politically and theologically, they revealed how congregations in the 1960s had come to see the church as an urban, social institution, rather than strictly a spiritual haven.

For example, in the 1950s when mainline Protestant churches considered whether to relocate to the suburbs, Christ Episcopal Church, Indianapolis's most affluent church located on the Circle in the center of downtown, decided to stay put. The decision was strongly affected by Eli Lilly, the church's most prominent member, who in 1953 gave a one-million-dollar gift to Christ Episcopal with the requirement that the "income be used to maintain the church in repair and continue its ministry to the community if the congregation could not afford to do so."[25] Lilly also suggested that Christ Episcopal be designated the diocesan cathedral to further secure the downtown location. Notwithstanding the significance of Lilly's gift, congregants knew that it was impossible to remain in the city without addressing the monumental demographic changes around them. Most of Christ Episcopal's members witnessed the urban transformation as they drove in from the northern side of the city or from the new northern suburbs.

National Episcopal leaders who played a prominent role in the larger urban ministry movement also affected local Episcopalians. The national Episcopal Church's Joint Urban Program sponsored conferences to raise "consciousness" about "urban issues" and supported the Chicago-based Urban Training Center for clergy. In 1964 the Episcopal Church founded the periodical *Church in the Metropolis,* which, as its name suggests, encouraged critical thought about the church's role in the city.[26]

Christ Episcopal was well positioned to participate in this national movement because its members had always been an integral part of Indianapolis's civic life. It counted among its members prominent businessmen with positions of economic power and a propensity for civic engagement. Their wives were no less active, attending to activities that guaranteed Christ Episcopal social respectability. Christ Episcopal was clearly a historic civic church where city leaders met to create and maintain the social, economic, and political networks that defined the city.

Christ Episcopal's outreach activity revealed its new sensibility as an urban, rather than civic, church. Like other mainline Protestant churches, it had since its nineteenth-century origin been concerned for the spiritual lives of "unchurched" children. In 1959, Christ

Episcopal established Cathedral House "to serve many of the less fortunate families living within a 10-block area near the downtown church."[27] Cathedral House offered religious services for children and a kindergarten. Just six years later, the congregation's concerns toward the social needs of the neighborhood had changed dramatically. Christ Episcopal played a central role in the formation of Episcopal Community Services (ECS), at 1557 Central Street, that offered emergency food, after-school tutorials, a job service program, and a clothing pantry. In addition to its fifty regular volunteer workers, Episcopal Community Services had a paid staff of five, including a full-time psychiatrist and a social caseworker.[28] ECS, like most Episcopal initiatives across the nation, was constrained by the fact that "the church has an easier time trying to abate poverty through direct service rather than dealing with issues of race and class as causal factors." Still, Christ Episcopal congregants did move beyond former evangelical goals and learn that the city had problems the church could not ignore.[29] Canon Frank V. H. Carthy, the executive director, suggested ECS was not simply a traditional charity. "We're not a do-good organization. We're here to meet the emotional and physical needs of people."[30]

Not all churches that relocated to suburbs broke all ties to the city. When First Presbyterian moved from downtown and merged with Meridian Heights Presbyterian Church at 47th and Central Street, it retained ownership of its former building—renamed Metro Church—to provide social services to the neighborhood whose residents had never been members. With assistance from the Presbytery, Metro Church thrived. It offered day care and a clothing bank as well as mental health services. Metro Center also welcomed secular groups such as the Welfare Rights Organization to meet in its building.[31]

Fletcher Place Church, in contrast to Christ Episcopal and Metro Church, was a historic "urban church" which had always had a strong social mission. Since the early twentieth century it had offered social, educational, and health programs to nonmembers at the Fletcher Place Community Center. When Miller Newton became head pastor in 1963, he transformed Fletcher Place into one of Indianapolis's most politically active, progressive urban churches.

Newton recognized the importance of health clinics, gymnasiums, and day nurseries, but he also brought neighborhood residents, among the poorest in the city, together to speak out and organize. This was particularly important for Fletcher Place Church, whose neighborhood, populated by poor whites with Appalachian roots, suffered from "high [levels of] crime and juvenile delinquency" as well as "high unemployment."[32] Neighborhood residents did not have access to political resources and had become alienated from religious institutions. In addition to participating in city-wide conflicts over the War on Poverty, Newton reached out to his neighbors. He went to what he called the "natural meeting places of life—homes, service stations, soda shops, and to street corners—" to learn about the people in his community.[33] Newton created the Outpost, a storefront church in a tough area of his southeast neighborhood, where he conducted "informal meetings," or "conversations" as he called them, rather than church services.[34] At the Outpost, Newton hoped men and women would voice their perspectives, find a place within the church, and nurture the political will to challenge inequalities and injustices. Some residents did, in fact, form neighborhood block groups and protest slum housing and poor health inspections."[35]

Thus, Indianapolis's most prominent Episcopal church and two of its oldest Presbyterian and Methodist churches were among the earliest proponents of urban ministry, like liberal Protestants across the nation. Some conservative Protestants, however, also focused on the city to address pressing urban issues, though their framing of and solutions for the problems diverged from those of their liberal counterparts.

In Indianapolis, the Salvation Army encouraged the development of the Shack, an urban ministry for teenagers. Salvation Army members saw how the enticing secular culture lured Indianapolis's teenagers more effectively than did churches. But instead of lamenting the waywardness of youth and the corrupting influence of the larger culture, the Shack adapted the secular adolescent culture to its own evangelical principles and goals to attract the young. The Shack employed a young staff hip to teen pop culture and skilled at employing popular cultural images within a conservative religious framework. The Shack sponsored dances, played rock and roll, and had a pool table. The recreational rooms at the Shack's center as well as the Shack's bus, used to transport kids to summer outings, were painted in psychedelic colors. When asked why teens came to the Shack, one worker explained how the center was known as a psychedelic and "swinging" place. Some Salvation Army members who "frowned on the dancing and some of the other activities" initially expressed concern, but the Shack's success muted critical voices.[36] In the summer of 1971, 360 teens were regular members. Along with the staff, they helped make the Shack an integral part of Stringtown, conducting neighborhood clean-ups, providing job counseling and placement, and sponsoring recreational activities.

The involvement of the Shack, Christ Episcopal, Metro Church, and Fletcher Place in urban ministries demonstrated the theological and political diversity of the movement. They all, however, identified strongly with their neighborhoods. Both the Shack and the Outpost were vocal about neighborhood boundaries, communicating their missions to serve residents. They sent out weekly newsletters to every home in their respective neighborhoods with information about their centers. In addition, the Fletcher Place Community Center required that staff "live in the community area."[37] The Shack had no such residential requirement, but its leaders were nonetheless proud that "the majority [of its paid staff] is from the neighborhood."[38] Although Cathedral House did not restrict its services to those in the immediate neighborhood, it did consider the area around 16th and Central Street as its "area of most intense social service."[39]

Community organizations quickly learned the importance of identifying with and understanding their neighborhoods. When the Presbyterian Mayer Chapel decided to develop an urban focus in 1962, it asked the Community Service Council to conduct a study of its southeastside neighborhood. In response to that study, Mayer conducted its own house-to-house survey to get "to know more intimately the families served and a plan to meet their needs."[40] Ten years later Mayer's thriving center included health clinics, a Planned Parenthood, and a Welfare Rights Organization. Mayer was not unique. When the Assumption Catholic Church sought a better understanding of its neighborhood, parishioners did their own door-to-door survey to interview residents and collect "sociological data" on both Catholic and non-Catholic families.[41]

Reverend Lewis Deer, head of the Broadway Christian Center, was one of Indianapolis's more vocal proponents of neighborhood awareness. He believed urban ministries should offer more than religious instruction and fellowship; they should also tackle secular issues such as "traffic, police action, housing, schools, or employment." At Broadway, he emphasized, "what happens in the neighborhood is the primary concern." Deer did not think Broadway exceptional, but instead characterized it as "an outgrowth of the changing neighborhood concept as expressed by many inner city churches."[42] Deer, like other urban clergy, believed urban ministry must transform relations between clergy and laity. He rejected the idea that the "man in the pulpit makes the difference," and argued for a leading role for the laity. Urban ministry must act as a "directing agency, coalescing local sentiment and feeling."[43] The new neighborhood focus, then, meant not only that religious communities had an obligation to understand social ills within the context of their neighborhoods, but that they must be attentive to the concerns of the residents in those neighborhoods.

Clergy generally embraced these progressive ideas more readily than the laity. In Indianapolis and across the nation in the 1960s, clergy were more politically active and liberal than their congregations were.[44] Clergy could not take lay support for granted, but instead had to convince congregants that a church with an urban mission must be concerned first and foremost with providing services and addressing community issues rather than traditional evangelization. Dr. Bryon Stroh of North Methodist was especially direct, informing his congregants that "we must give the help that is needed in a neighborhood and not expect that those helped will necessarily attend our church."[45] Like Stroh, Anthony Thurston, executive secretary of the Urban Mission Council of Indianapolis, forthrightly declared, "Our purpose is to serve the neighborhoods around the church with no restrictions as to denominations." This was especially important when dealing with children, who "don't want religion shoved down them" and "prefer recreation over religion."[46]

To justify urban ministry, clergy highlighted practical issues. Reverend C. William Bryan, pastor of Central Christian, claimed the urban church must differentiate itself from its suburban counterpart in order to attract former city residents back for religious services. "If we had not had strong programs relating to the community—if we had just served ourselves instead—we would have died."[47] For Bryan, whose church was located in the heart of downtown, serving the larger community was also a moral issue with theological roots. "We just couldn't justify staying here on this very expensive corner if we didn't involve the neighborhood." Christ Episcopal, also in the downtown business district, was dependent on a membership driving in from long distances, and it confronted similar issues. Asked whether the members of Christ Episcopal "mind this disproportionate share of time and money spent on nonmembers," Canon Charles Gibson replied, "If they resented it, they couldn't call themselves Christians."[48]

Although the clergy who initiated urban ministries sometimes worried that they were calling on their people to tread on unknown territory, many churches already had long histories of urban engagement. During the late nineteenth and early twentieth centuries, most Protestant denominations actively supported city missions and missionary societies, which were an integral part of the urban religious landscape.[49] However, the urban ministries of the 1960s differed from those older missions. Progressive Era city missionaries assumed that it was their responsibility to bring Catholic and Jewish immigrants into the Protestant fold and thereby save their souls and shape their emerging American identities. Turn-of-the-century urban missionaries also hoped their missions would become self-supporting churches. In contrast, in the 1960s, urban clergy who instituted urban ministries were more concerned with addressing secular issues and less certain about the means to achieve their goals.

It was one thing to extol the value of "listening" to the community; it was another matter to successfully institute such a practice. In cities such as Chicago and New York, political and civic leaders had historically been forced to recognize a plurality of voices. In Indianapolis, by contrast, dissent and debate were historically not part of the political culture. Indianapolis lacked the religious and ethnic diversity that in other cities made competing interests and conflict impossible to avoid. In Indianapolis, business and civic leaders embraced the notion that a unitary common good could be easily identified.

This kind of conservatism found structural form in 1969 under Mayor Richard Lugar when Indianapolis adopted a system of governance called Unigov. Under Unigov, the city's political boundaries were extended from Center Township to include all nine outlying townships. Consequently, Indianapolis's geographic area increased ninefold and most of the city's suburbs became part of the city proper. Not all services were combined, however. School districts remained part of township governance. An expression of the belief that all in Indianapolis shared common interests and envisioned common solutions to urban problems, Unigov in fact generated black protest. African Americans saw in Unigov a scheme to dilute the power of the Democratic Party and African Americans. Although Republicans denied the charge, it took more than thirty years for another Democrat to win the mayoralty.

While competing interests were downplayed, Indianapolis's older social welfare institutions wanted to become more responsive to their clients. For example, at Christamore House, a settlement established by the Disciples of Christ in the early twentieth century, the white middle-class women in charge had difficulty identifying with their black westside neighborhood in the 1950s. Local residents complained they had no power over the programs or policies at Christamore, which operated without knowledge of the neighborhood.[50] The Community Service Council agreed and criticized Christamore for failing in its responsibility to "know what their neighborhoods desire and offer programs geared to meet such needs, not needs which the staff might believe the neighborhood has."[51] Christamore House was not alone. Fletcher Place members also worried that they were failing to listen carefully to the concerns of the poor who lived in their neighborhood even though Newton was the most progressive and outspoken clergyman in the city.

In addition to theological and political issues, institutional and structural issues also affected the dimensions, longevity, and vitality of urban ministries. For example, when Third Christian (Disciples of Christ) moved from 17th Street and Broadway to 5220 East Fall Creek in 1962, the congregation launched urban programs in its former building. For eight years, the congregation offered job training and housed government-sponsored War on Poverty activities. In the early 1970s, however, the center closed. Reverend Ernest Thompson explained: "We attempted a social ministry there after we left, but frankly the expense of operating the program became prohibitive. You see, we're autonomous and don't have any mission board support, so we didn't have any choice." Thompson compared his experience with First Presbyterian, which had merged with Meridian Heights after its move north of the city. First Presbyterian had "left behind the . . . Metropolitan Center—a denomination-sponsored social action project that included more than twenty services from day care to draft counseling." Thompson claimed that the Presbytery covered 80 percent of Metro Center's $100,000 budget while only 20 percent came from the congregation.[52] Thus, Presbytery funds enabled First Presbyterian, even after it had moved, to engage in urban ministry on a scale out of the reach of independent congregations absent strong denominational structures. Other congregations, whose denominations lacked funds for urban ministries, encountered the same obstacles as Third Christian. The Christian Methodist Episcopal Church, too "impoverished to give funds and personnel," limited the effectiveness of Bishop Joseph C. Coles's urban ministry in Harlem, New York.[53] Likewise, American Baptists "did not possess the staff and financial resources to match the larger mainline Protestant denominations."[54]

Ecumenism and Geographical Boundaries

In the 1960s, both liberal and conservative churches faced a variety of challenges in instituting urban ministry programs. The new urban awareness that drove clergy and laity to reach out to their less privileged neighbors also affected the relations among religious institutions. More specifically, as churches from various denominations holding different theological worldviews confronted similar urban issues, they began in increasing numbers to collaborate in ecumenical associations defined by geographical boundaries.

In 1957 the city had ten territory-based ministerial associations. However, few clergy who belonged to those associations placed much emphasis on the significance of the regional boundaries. The only specifically "neighborhood-defined" association was Irvington. By 1972, however, the number of geographically defined ministerial associations had increased to twenty-six, and most were neighborhood-based with strong geographical identities.[55] While some associations met infrequently and did not do much beyond issuing joint pamphlets announcing Sunday services, others became very active in their neighborhoods and had ambitious goals. One such group was Operation Prove It, an organization of seventeen near-northside churches that focused attention on dilapidated housing, juvenile delinquency, interracial tensions, and job insecurity. Another was the "Southwest Order of the Fish," a group of seven churches that provided emergency care including babysitting and meals "to anybody who needs it."[56] Riley-Lockerbie Ministerial Association, a group of nine historic downtown congregations, was one of the most visible. These nine churches attended to the "personal problems of residents," ran a preschool, a clothing bank, and provided services for the elderly."[57] Like many other pastoral groups, Riley-Lockerbie served the less privileged and judged its success not by the number of people it brought into the fold but by the impact that its social programs had on the quality of life in the city. The secular concerns that drove ecumenical efforts were most clearly seen in 1968 when Catholic, Jewish, and Protestant groups, including the Indiana Catholic Conference, the Christian Inner City Association, and the Indianapolis Council of Churches, met to devise the "Metropolitan Legislative Program" to demand greater public assistance for women who received AFDC.[58]

In addition to participating in ecumenical pastoral associations, many clergy assumed leading roles in secular neighborhood associations and organizations. Father James Kohls, who participated in the formation of the United Southeast Community Organization (USCO), was one of many clergy who helped shape the agendas of the emerging neighborhood associations. The War on Poverty drew the attention of numerous clergy. Robert W. Koenig, the president of the Church Federation during most of the 1960s, sat on the board of Community Action Against Poverty between 1968 and 1971, but he was not alone. Other clergy who served on the board included Reverend Robert Smith, Father George Elford, Reverend Ray Sells, Reverend Mozell Sanders, Reverend William Clark, and Reverend J. Soloman.[59]

That clergy would decide to become involved in secular and even governmental initiatives to attack urban ills was not surprising. When encouraging the development of ministerial neighborhood groups, the Church Federation suggested strongly that they be "patterned in accordance with present and developing neighborhood association boundaries."[60] The Church Federation even helped organize several secular community organizations including NESCO (Northeast Side Community Organization), USSCO (United South Side Community Organization), NWCO (Northwest Community Organization) and USCO (the United Southeast Community Organization)—all of which used federal community block grants for community development projects.[61]

These various interdenominational and neighborhood-based associations helped further educate clergy about the needs of the city and propelled the more liberal to become involved in organizations with an explicitly political focus. The most active was the Christian Inner City Association, which, as chapter 3 describes, closely scrutinized governmental figures who refused to acknowledge, let alone address, the city's class and racial injustices. The CICA, which included Fletcher Place's Miller Newton as a leading member, tackled such issues as housing, racial discrimination, and voting by issuing public statements and lobbying at the state and federal level for changes in government policy. The local chapter of the Southern Christian Leadership Conference, an affiliate of the national organization headed by Martin Luther King, Jr., focused primarily on racial justice issues but was no less active or vocal in its criticism of governmental policies. These more outspoken organizations frequently earned the ire of conservative forces and were ignored by moderates.

Housing

Indianapolis, a city that shunned combative politics, placed limits on acceptable protest. No religious group felt these limitations more strongly than the Church Federation, whose membership included moderates and conservatives. Even as it moved beyond traditional evangelism and encouraged engagement with urban social and economic changes, the Church Federation wanted to keep its broad-based support. This led the Federation and its Urban Task Force to take up the issue of housing for the poor, a ministry that would not divide its membership. When the Federation addressed Indianapolis's housing crisis, it sought to use the resources of government on behalf of the poor.

Despite Indianapolis's high rate of home ownership, affordable housing had long been a problem. Between 1945 and 1961, the Indianapolis Redevelopment Commission (IRC) spent $10 million to "combat the slum problems" of the inner city, but it failed to attend to the needs of the displaced.[62] For example, when it razed 500 low-income homes downtown to make room for Riley Towers, an upscale high-rise apartment complex, the IRC never adequately responded to the poor who were forced out.

Urban housing problems became acute in the 1960s when the city razed neighborhoods to make way for highways I-65 and I-465 and the new state university, Indiana University–Purdue University Indianapolis (IUPUI), just southeast of downtown. At the time, city planners estimated that the 30,000 people displaced would need 11,000 rental units and 2,400 owner-occupied units.[63] Because the displaced tended to be the poor, those least able to afford housing found themselves scrambling for new homes.

Despite the gravity of the situation, authorities failed to respond adequately in large part because the city was reluctant to provide public housing. Indianapolis's only public housing—a well-designed complex of low-rise buildings on the southeast side—was built in the 1930s. However, support for public housing had withered after the New Deal when Indianapolis took pride in its refusal to accept many kinds of federal funding. In the 1950s newspapers ran articles touting Indiana for not participating in the growing welfare state. As a result, between 1952 and 1964, years when the city underwent massive change, the Indianapolis Housing Authority built no new public housing.[64] Exacerbating the situation, a large portion of the existing Lockfield public housing project was torn down to make room for IUPUI.

Although the Church Federation was aware of the housing problems, it did not want to pursue policies deemed politically controversial. In 1964, when the City-County Council voted on a proposed open housing bill, the Federation refused to support it.[65] The Federation, unlike religious organizations in other cities that supported public housing, remained conspicuously silent even when Homes Before Highways and the Christian Inner City Association protested the city's housing policies through public pronouncements.

The Church Federation, however, was not completely inactive. It participated in the Mayor's Commission on Human Rights, which held a housing conference in June 1966, and one year later, the Federation sponsored its own conference on housing at Mt. Zion Church, where more than 100 participants discussed the widespread problem with run-down housing. Participants learned that 18.2 percent of all housing and 33.5 percent of all housing for blacks was substandard.[66] After the conference, the Federation called on individual churches to identify housing for the underprivileged and share that information with the Church Federation, which would act as a clearinghouse. Unfortunately, only sixty clergy responded. A more organized approach was needed.[67]

The Church Federation's limited response demonstrated the constraints the city's conservative political climate and the diversity among its own membership placed upon it. However, when the U.S. Congress passed legislation making it easier for nonprofits to receive public funds for social services, the Church Federation responded enthusiastically, confident that it would finally have the opportunity to confront housing issues in a manner that its members would embrace.

The 1967 amendments to the Social Security Act, Title IV-A, encouraged states to use federal money to purchase services from private contractors. Before this amendment, most federal social service dollars had been channeled to public agencies. Title IV-A gave states financial incentive to turn to the nonprofit sector, promising to match every dollar raised locally with three federal dollars.[68] Other federal programs instituted in the late 1960s and 1970s, including block grants and FHA subsidies, also increased the flow of federal money to nonprofits. Particularly important was the rent supplement program that required tenants to pay 25 percent of their income for rent, while the federal government paid the difference between rent paid and fair market value.[69] For a city that valued private responses to public problems and had long been resistant to dependence on public funds, these amendments to the Social Security Act were welcomed. Indianapolis residents agreed that if the federal government appropriated tax funds for social services, the state should have the power to channel those funds through nonprofits rather than government agencies.

Religious groups in Indianapolis increasingly sought public responses to social ills. In 1968 the Church Federation encouraged Indiana congressmen to support the federal Housing Act to address the housing crisis. The Federation also established Housing Opportunities Multiplied Ecumenically (HOME), a nonprofit made up of sixty-five churches, to provide low-income housing. HOME was confident that poor people would be eager to occupy housing provided by churches. When Meridian St. Methodist Church renovated a single house into a five-unit apartment building, it was "besieged with people."[70] Mt. Zion Church, which used a FHA mortgage to build a forty-unit building at 34th and Boulevard in the northwest corner of the city, was also successful.[71]

Before HOME began its own rehabilitation projects, its members traveled to national conferences on housing and visited successful religious nonprofits in other cities. Aware of its participation in a national trend, HOME began its first rehabilitation project, Hometown 1, to convert eight homes into multi-family units for thirty-nine families.

Federal rent subsidies of $180,000 and an FHA 3 percent, forty-year loan financed Hometown 1. Located in the 2400 block of Central Avenue on the northwest side, Hometown 1 served families displaced due to highway construction and the building of IUPUI. HOME wanted to serve those least able to secure housing on their own. The first residents of Hometown 1 included a large number of women who received AFDC. The first twenty-two families included many households headed by single mothers; forty-three of the eighty-five children in Hometown 1 were under the age of five.[72]

Members of HOME understood their housing venture as a central part of the Church Federation's commitment to urban ministry. They wanted to provide more than just shelter. As one participant described it, HOME was dedicated to "serv[ing] the whole man" and building strong community-based neighborhoods.[73] To meet the needs of residents, HOME planned to offer counseling, "crisis intervention casework," job counseling, health care, and day care. "Unless we meet all the needs of our tenants we cannot expect to create the feeling that this is a neighborhood on its way up."[74] HOME officials hoped that once the needs of individuals were met, "people would really get to know each other, develop a feeling of mutual responsibility and a sense of community."[75] HOME wanted to "help residents think through and find solutions for neighborhood problems" by "conversing [with them] at the grass-roots level," not by telling them what to do.[76] According to HOME, "genuine rehabilitation" is a "matter of neighborhoods rather than individual buildings."[77]

In addition to providing direct services to residents and cultivating neighborhood ties, HOME hoped also to muster the clout to improve the infrastructures of the city's dilapidated neighborhoods by convincing public authorities to close designated streets, build playgrounds, repave streets, and build community centers.[78] In 1971 they put forward an estimated budget of $2 million for renewal of the city's infrastructure.[79] The city refused to entertain the request, but the fact that HOME officials even made such a demand demonstrated their cognizance of structural problems and the sum of public money needed to solve them.

Other religious nonprofits had similar goals and practices. Interfaith Housing, a spin-off of the Christian Inner City Association, focused on the rehabilitation of single-family housing and provided counseling to the residents. In addition, Interfaith Housing helped organize two inner-city block groups, hoping, like HOME, to empower residents and create a sense of community.[80]

Although HOME was a nonprofit with ties to the Church Federation, it always remained conscious that "the FHA made possible a level of response that was heretofore economically impossible for us."[81] When HOME did try to raise private funds, it failed miserably. In 1969 HOME decided to create a privately funded endowment. The Lilly Endowment gave a $60,000 three-year grant to cover administrative costs, expecting that the gift would encourage private beneficence from others.[82] Despite HOME's hopes of raising $100,000, the city's churches contributed a mere $12,500.[83] The key to HOME's success came from government: rent supplements and FHA low-interest loans.[84]

HOME was not unique in its dependence on federal funds. Political scientists have described how the number of nonprofits climbed across the nation as a result of the introduction of federal funds. Between 1965 and 1970, federal appropriations for social services grew from $812 million to $2.2 billion, including a significant increase for nonprofits. The War on Poverty's community action agencies of the mid-1960s were early beneficiaries of such practices, but other independent nonprofits benefited as well.

Public Funds and New Opportunities

Federal funding that spurred the creation of new nonprofits also allowed older ones to expand their reach. In Indianapolis no organization was more profoundly affected by federal funding than Catholic Charities. In the late 1960s, for the first time in the history of Catholic Charities, the number of people receiving assistance from the agency declined. For instance, the number of children placed in foster homes fell from 205 in 1962 to 32 in 1968.[85] At a time when urban policy makers focused on neighborhoods, Catholic Charities offered the same centralized city services it had provided in the 1940s. In 1966, national Catholic leaders conducted a formal review and criticized Catholic Charities in Indianapolis for not exploiting parishes to shape neighborhood life and for not instituting programs to empower the poor.

Catholic Charities of Indianapolis was aware that it stood at a crossroads. If Catholic Charities wanted to remain a vibrant force, it needed to offer new services and focus on neighborhood life. This was a difficult challenge. We have seen how individual Catholic clergy and parishes had begun to think about the Catholics' obligation to the city, with Father Strange and Faye Williams leading the way. They used St. Rita's to host War on Poverty programs, and they spoke out against urban inequalities. They were joined by Reverend Donald Schmidlin of Catholic Charities, who criticized the city's treatment of the poor and the punitive practices of the Township Trustees. However, Catholic Charities as a social service organization found it hard to change. Although members had discussed a "strong counseling program and parish centered social work" and had described how many "parishes are beginning to see the need for greater involvement in community and neighborhood development and organization," they also lamented their lack of "funds" and "trained personnel for such a job."[86]

In 1973 Catholic Charities finally began serious parish-based work. It established a Neighborhood Community Services Program, later renamed the Parish Outreach Program (POP). The first churches to offer services were St. Andrew's, Holy Trinity, and Little Flower. Catholic Charities wanted to learn about Indianapolis's urban parishes and help them reach out to their neighborhoods. Its central premise was that "each of these parishes has a relatively unique character, . . . concerns, problems and needs." As such, community consultants who instituted the new program introduced the parish to the "neighborhood associations within the parish boundaries" and urged collaboration with those associations. At St. Andrew's, for example, the consultant arranged a meeting between the director of the local CAAP multi-service center and a "representative of the parish administration."[87]

By 1979, twelve additional parishes were offering services. To support them, Catholic Charities was receiving $67,000 from the federal government, up from less than $20,000 in the mid-1970s.[88] POP's growth, in part the result of Catholics' desire to exert influence over their parish neighborhoods, cannot be explained without reference to the policies of the federal government. Catholic Charities took advantage of the availability of Title X funds from the federal government to expand their influence in the city.

Government money also affected in a fundamental way the mission of Catholic Charities. Until the mid-1970s, Catholic Charities of Indianapolis served Catholics almost exclusively. Even though the Second Vatican Council (1962–1965) articulated a theological rationale for Catholics to reach out to non-Catholics, few Catholics in Indianapolis acted on those ideals. One result was that African Americans, generally not Catholic, received few services from Catholic Charities. Only when federal money *required* Catholic Charities to serve non-Catholics did the organization take as its mission the goal of working "beyond religious boundaries."[89] Once Catholic Charities began working with non-Catholics, however, it took great pride in its outreach to all faiths. By 1980, POP served a largely poor, black, non-Catholic population. For example, one-half of the families who sought counseling from Catholic Charities also received AFDC, and one third were black. Only 26 percent of all clients were Catholic.[90] The nondiscriminatory conditions tied to government money gave Catholics an opportunity to develop a new relationship with city authorities as well as with the poorest, most vulnerable citizens. The restrictions placed by the government on federal funding compelled Catholics to abide by the church's new theological ideals.

Catholic Charities and HOME were not the only organizations to benefit from federal funds. Smaller organizations also hoped to leverage public resources and believed such assistance would aid them in their quest to help revitalize the city. In the early 1970s, when the Presbytery cut off funds, Mayer House—a community center that offered health clinics and a thrift shop and sponsored a Welfare Rights Organization—turned to the board of Community Action Against Poverty for money.[91] So too did Broadway Christian Center, which had initially been supported by the United Church Missionary Society and the Association of Christian Churches.[92] Limited private funding also led Immanuel Church, which operated the Immanuel Counseling Center, to seek more than $68,000 from the mayor's Community Service Program. Dependent on private funds to support its day care center and after-school program, Immanuel Church wanted public money to offer counseling to low-income people who lived at Beechwood Garden, a housing project. In its proposal, Immanuel Church stated that the "counseling will be available on personality problems, religious questions, interpersonal relations and crisis counseling."[93]

Hope Unfulfilled

Urban ministries in the 1960s and early 1970s began with energy and optimism. The dedicated religious leaders and laity who participated in such ventures truly believed it was within their reach to help solve the problems of urban America. However, few possessed the ability or resources to fully realize their goals.

HOME encountered many obstacles in its quest to create cohesive communities. In the neighborhoods where HOME rehabilitated apartment houses, residents who owned homes in those areas feared their new poor, black neighbors. At Hometown 1, nearby homeowners alleged that the children who lived in the apartments roamed the neighborhood without parental oversight and that the grounds surrounding the renovated buildings were run-down. Teachers at the Montessori Academy grew particularly angry. They complained that residents at Hometown 1 were "not good neighbors," "play loud music," and "don't dispose of their garbage properly."[94] Although such charges might be dismissed as bigotry against the poor, HOME did in fact encounter trouble with its new residents. At their meetings, HOME officials discussed how their tenants often failed to pay their rent on time, damaged property, and left litter strewn inside and outside the buildings. Even more disturbing were reports of "children running rampant" and rising crime rates.[95]

As HOME struggled with its role as property manager, relations with the FHA soured. The FHA had guaranteed the loans HOME received for its first two large-scale projects, a sum just under $2 million.[96] But when HOME submitted an application for a third project in 1972, the FHA rejected it. The FHA was alarmed that, after HOME announced its intention to begin a third development, residents in the proposed neighborhood began to sell their homes, and the price of housing fell. The FHA also expressed concern about the cost-effectiveness of rehabilitating older buildings—which it claimed was often as expensive as new construction.[97]

The withdrawal of FHA support presented an insurmountable obstacle for HOME if it hoped to continue to offer low-cost housing. Equally discouraging, however, was the fact that HOME never realized its goal of creating cohesive communities supported by strong social support systems. The city never appropriated funds for infrastructure improvement, and money never became available for social services such as social workers and day care centers. HOME had begun its ministry acknowledging that social programs were necessary to serve the "whole man." Only reluctantly did HOME admit, despite its best intentions, that "tenants in scattered sites seem to have little consciousness of community."[98]

Surprised at its mission's failure to reach its goals and bombarded with public hostility, HOME shifted its focus to the elderly. Citing "problems with family housing," HOME's director stated optimistically that homes for the elderly would be "welcomed by the neighborhood." He added, "The government is interested in it" and "its chances of success were better." Reflecting on the past three years, the president noted, "we have tackled the toughest" and now it is time to "go to something with less risk." Serving the elderly would also have the added advantage of "increas[ing] credibility with the churches."[99]

When the federal government began to fund nonprofits in 1967, public officials believed that nonprofits could help solve the problems of urban America. The nation still relies heavily on them to deliver social services. Supporters of this relationship argue that nonprofits are more responsive to those they serve, less entangled by bureaucratic webs, and more innovative than public agencies. Whether or not these claims are true, the story of religious nonprofits in Indianapolis during the 1960s and 1970s demonstrates some of the limitations of such social welfare policies.

In particular, the experiences of HOME and Catholic Charities demonstrate all too clearly the costs and risks associated with such relationships both for nonprofits and the underprivileged they served. HOME never had sufficient funding to implement its mission, and once the federal government decided to cut funding, HOME had no way to continue its work with the poorest. Catholic Charities found itself in a similar situation when in the early 1980s it was forced to dismantle POP. The Ombudsman Act, passed with the support of President Ronald Reagan, eliminated Title XX, which had provided states with matching funds, and severely cut back on appropriations for community action agencies and health clinics. The overall effect was that federal spending on social services declined in real terms by almost 50 percent between 1980 and 1990.[100] Steven Rathgeb Smith and Michael Lipsky have pointed out that one of the great ironies of the government's use of nonprofits to expand social services in the late 1960s was that "the cuts of the Reagan-Bush years were facilitated by the very flexibility which supported the contracting system during its years of growth."[101]

Considering the public fanfare surrounding the creation of HOME, it might be expected that the shift to housing for the elderly would have created a great stir among the poor and advocates of the poor. However, the poor who benefited from HOME never protested the shift. Nonprofits, regardless of how dependent on government funds they might be, are ultimately beholden to the private citizens who run them, not to the citizenry as a whole. These contracting relations have implications for the meaning of citizenship in a democracy. When a nonprofit decides to change focus or disband altogether, citizens who depend on its services usually accept such changes with little protest because they see the publicly funded service as a voluntary gift, not a government entitlement or a right of citizenship.

The story of urban ministry in the 1960s and 1970s is a bittersweet one. Religious groups were extremely enthusiastic about the possibility of transforming the city, and politically progressive ministers received media attention. After 1967 the federal government began to fund enthusiastic religious groups. However, with the exception of large organizations with tested histories—such as Catholic Charities and the Salvation Army—few urban ministries, even those receiving public funds, survived. Describing the church-based urban training centers that emerged across the nation in the 1960s, Clifford J. Green notes, "The rapid emergence of these training centers and programs is as striking as the fact that most of them flourished and died in fifteen years."[102] The same could be said of urban ministries more generally. During the 1970s and 1980s urban ministries that began with high hopes were shut down, including ECS and Mayer House.

As urban ministries shut down, religious institutions lost interest in urban problems. This was even true of the Church Federation. Although it continues as an important force in the city, it is no longer recognized as a force to solve social problems. Equally striking were the changes in institutions such as Fletcher Place Community Center. Its intense political activism of the 1960s has given way to a low-profile focus on social services. These stories offer lessons for policy makers in the twenty-first century who are looking to congregations to solve social ills.

V

"ONE SOUL AT A TIME": WELFARE REFORM AND FAITH-BASED ORGANIZATIONS

When Stephen Goldsmith became the mayor of Indianapolis in 1992, he promised to increase the role of the private sector in providing city services and thus to "reinvent government." Motivated by the belief that "public resources foster local solutions best when the programs use market mechanisms," Goldsmith, during his eight years in office, increased dramatically the number of private companies receiving government contracts. He cut the city payroll for nonsafety public employees by more than 50 percent and the overall public payroll by more than 27 percent.[1] To deal with social problems and revitalize the city, Goldsmith called on the churches. He justified the shift to religious institutions with the assertion that he was merely asking churches to provide the social service work they had done before the expanding welfare state had squeezed them out. "We realize that the true grassroots method to reforming welfare is through the community of faith, not government."[2] By the time Goldsmith left office in 2000, Indianapolis had achieved national recognition for its use of religious organizations to confront crime-ridden neighborhoods and assist former welfare recipients.

When George W. Bush made "compassionate conservatism" the central theme of his 2000 presidential campaign—telling the nation that his administration "will look first to faith-based organizations" to solve social problems—he singled out Indianapolis as a model.³ One of the first places he spoke about his ideas was in Indianapolis where, before the Front Porch Alliance in early 1999, Bush endorsed government funding of faith-based organizations.⁴ Like Goldsmith, Bush exclaimed with certainty that faith-based organizations were "effective" and "have clear advantages over government."⁵ As president, to win support for the Charity, Aid, Recovery, and Empowerment Act, Bush explained to religious and nonprofit leaders invited to the White House that their support for faith-based organizations was essential. "Government can write checks, but it can't put hope in people's hearts, or a sense of purpose in people's lives. That is done by people of faith who have heard a call and who act on faith and are willing to share that faith."⁶

For the first time, Indianapolis had been recognized as a leader in national social welfare trends. This attention did *not* demonstrate how much Indianapolis had changed—the city had always privileged private over public initiatives—but *how much* the national goals and mood had changed. In the 1960s, leading social welfare experts saw poverty as a structural issue and assumed that government had a responsibility to provide a social safety net through government agencies or nonprofit organizations. These assumptions eroded in the 1970s and 1980s as public hostility to welfare mounted. By the late 1990s, when many Democrats and most Republicans agreed that large-scale public assistance programs ought to be abolished, they began to look to churches to solve social problems. This chapter examines faith-based programs in Indianapolis within this larger national context.

The monumental 1996 welfare reform act and the trend toward privatization of government functions help explain how and why politicians began to call on churches to play a greater, if not primary, role in the provision of social services.

When Bill Clinton became president, he fulfilled his campaign promise to "end welfare as we know it." However, after Congress refused to support Clinton's proposals to reform the nation's public assistance program, conservative Republicans proposed their own, much more severe, welfare reform initiative, which Clinton signed into law on the eve of the 1996 presidential election.[7] This welfare bill, officially titled the Personal Responsibility and Work Opportunity Reconciliation Act, dismantled the federal program Aid to Families with Dependent Children (AFDC), in operation since 1935, and replaced it with Temporary Assistance to Needy Families (TANF).[8] Under AFDC, the federal government had provided matching funds to the states, which were then required to provide cash assistance to unemployed single parents with children under age eighteen. Although the amount each state provided to families varied greatly, the federal government provided at least some semblance of protection to those who received assistance. In contrast, under TANF, the states exercise almost complete control over whether and how funds are distributed. Each state receives block grants distributed to social service providers. In many states, public welfare agencies directly administer TANF funds and services. However, the states, if they choose, can contract with private agencies to provide those services. TANF money is not reserved solely for cash assistance, but can be used for an array of programs, including child care, drug rehabilitation, and job training.

Although the states enjoy latitude in deciding how to use TANF funds, the federal government imposes strict time limits on cash assistance to the poor. No recipient may receive more than two years of consecutive support and more than five years of lifetime support. States may choose to impose even more severe time restrictions. Thirteen states have imposed shorter lifetime limits, ranging from twenty-one to forty-eight months.[9]

Ever since President Franklin D. Roosevelt created AFDC as part of the New Deal, conservative forces had been intent on discrediting it. They expressed fear that public assistance created dependency and undermined the American values of liberty and independence.[10] Prior to the 1960s, however, the resentment directed at AFDC was contained because the larger culture promoted traditional gender roles. It was not popular to challenge the idea that mothers had a primary responsibility to tend to their children.

The political and cultural climate changed dramatically in the 1960s, when for the first time African American women in great numbers applied for and received AFDC. As welfare became racialized, opposition mounted.[11] The growing number of unwed mothers (both black and white) who did not give up their children for adoption but opted to raise them alone with AFDC support also troubled many Americans.[12] Although unintentionally, the women's movement of the 1970s also negatively affected public support for AFDC. As women demanded equal opportunity and treatment in the workplace, Americans wondered why they should support unwed women to stay home to care for their children. If married women were out in the workforce supporting their families, single mothers should be too. These factors together generated opposition to public assistance in the 1970s and 1980s.

By the 1990s, even liberal politicians had become disenchanted with this New Deal program, although the basis of their opposition varied from their conservative colleagues. Liberals lamented how payments were set so low that families lived in dire poverty. They feared that public welfare departments did little to help women who wanted to improve their lives through educational or vocational channels.

Not surprisingly, then, when in 1992 Bill Clinton told Americans he would overhaul the nation's welfare system, he won widespread support. However, not all were happy when the 1996 welfare reform act replaced the federal AFDC program with state-controlled TANF. Heated debate appropriately focused on the strict time limits the reform imposed on recipients. Religious groups, including the National Council of Churches, the National Conference of Catholic Bishops, and the Union of American Hebrew Congregations, opposed the bill most strongly.[13] They feared that the poor would no longer have a safety net and that the federal government was absolving itself of responsibility for the most vulnerable. Conservatives countered that the time restrictions were not unduly harsh and encouraged the poor to become self-sufficient.

The time limits revealed that many Americans accepted that the federal government has a limited obligation to the poorest citizens. The specific provisions for providing services reinforced that belief. Instead of permitting only government agencies to provide TANF services (as was the case with AFDC), the welfare reform act encouraged states to contract out services to the private sector. By allowing the states to shift responsibility for the poor to the private sector—both the nonprofit and for-profit arms—the federal government helped accelerate the process of privatization that had reconfigured government at all levels in the 1980s and 1990s.[14]

We need to carefully distinguish between the government "contracting out" for services and the recent trend toward "privatization." Since the 1960s the federal government has provided social services by giving contracts to nonprofits. The decision to establish those cooperative ventures was premised on the belief that organizations best able to provide services—whether they were governmental or private—should be mobilized. Some policy makers emphasized the financial advantage that would accrue. Others stressed the empowering impact such ventures would have on the nonprofit sector. Pragmatism rather than ideology ruled these policies during the 1960s and 1970s.[15]

While the more recent turn to privatization resembles in practice the "contracting out" policies established in the 1960s, the rhetoric, goals, and justification of those who tout privatization represent a new departure. Rather than considering which sector is best able to provide *specific* services, "privatizers" begin with the assumption that government is by definition unable to provide services efficiently and that public policies should be based on market axioms that rule economic life. As one commentator put it, advocates of privatization "assume that privatization will always and automatically achieve improved public service at a lower cost."[16] That they have been able to convince public authorities to shift responsibility for a wide range of services—including prisons, health care, and even in some cases public schools—to the private sector demonstrates just how popular such sentiments have become.

Privatization, however, involves more than just a search for efficiency and cost-effectiveness; it involves a reconsideration of the meaning of citizenship. Those who praise privatization, including former Mayor Goldsmith, commonly use market terms to describe the democratic process. When criticizing taxes and public spending Goldsmith stated, "Because government simply confiscates dollars rather than competing for them, government managers do not get information about their customers' needs and wants."[17] In Goldsmith's lexicon, citizens are "customers" and opinion polls are "customer surveys."[18] Running for Governor of Indiana in 1996, Goldsmith boasted, "For the last three years I've been CEO of Indianapolis. Now I'd like to privatize all of Indiana."[19]

The implications of employing market terms to describe and define democratic governance are far-reaching, especially for areas of human service such as social welfare and education. Quite often the higher principles and goals of education and social welfare conflict with market rules. Educating children and meeting the needs of the underprivileged are services that cannot be measured solely in terms of "cost-effectiveness" or "outputs." Echoing the sentiments of education reformers such as John Dewey, Professor Ellen Dannin has described how public education "is intended to do more than teach merely reading or writing or simply prepare students to join the workforce. It is intended to support our democracy by ensuring all citizens can take on the task of self-governance and to transmit a sense of shared identity."[20] Furthermore, excellent schools are expensive to run and so too are those social welfare programs that provide much-needed services such as child care and job training. However, as business goals and principles have come to define how Americans understand the commonwealth, it has become difficult to gain support for social programs whose benefits are not immediately evident or easily quantified.

Concurrent with this shift toward privatization, city mayors and state officials began to implement welfare reform in the 1990s. Rather than have public agencies institute welfare reforms, state and city governments looked to the nonprofit and for-profit sectors. As a result, today more so than at any other time in the past, public assistance is provided through a mix of all three sectors—government, nonprofit, and for-profit. However, the organizations politicians, including Goldsmith, are most eager to recruit are faith-based. Within the welfare reform act of 1996, there was a special provision called Charitable Choice, authored by Senator John Ashcroft of Missouri. Charitable Choice stipulated that when a state contracts out services to nongovernmental groups, religious organizations, including congregations, are free to compete for those contracts without compromising their "religious integrity." Charitable

Choice also stated that religious organizations are free to discriminate on the basis of religion in hiring. Proponents of Charitable Choice argue they are merely "leveling the playing field" for religious organizations.

The publicity surrounding Charitable Choice and President George W. Bush's Office of Faith-Based and Community Initiatives mistakenly make it appear as though religious organizations had previously been barred from government funding. On the contrary, for decades religious organizations such as Catholic Charities and Lutheran Family Social Services had received federal contracts.[21] The "domestic" peace corps, AmeriCorps, created by President Clinton, also relies heavily on faith-based organizations. During Clinton's administration, 6,000 of the 40,000 AmeriCorps programs were housed in religious institutions.[22] Prior to Charitable Choice, however, religious institutions receiving government money had to comply with federal civil rights employment statutes and the First Amendment's separation of church and state. Furthermore, congregations were not allowed to receive money directly. If a congregation wanted to receive government money or a government contract, it needed to establish a separate charitable organization. That organization was then expected to abide by the same rules as all other providers.

A firestorm erupted over the legality of Charitable Choice. Legal activists and scholars questioned the constitutionality of the federal civil rights employment exemption that allows faith-based organizations to discriminate on the basis of religion. They raised questions about the ambiguous, vaguely worded stipulation that religious organizations cannot be forced to compromise their "religious integrity." They have argued that this stipulation, as currently written, creates a context in which violations of the First Amendment are bound to occur.

Not all conservative religious groups have supported Charitable Choice. Speaking for the Baptist Joint Committee, Melissa Rodgers has warned that the idea of a "level playing field is dangerous," and religious institutions should be wary about it. She has described how the First Amendment recognizes that "religion is unique and must be treated differently by the government at times. Thus, it is sometimes subject to special limits (such as funding restrictions) and sometimes given special accommodations (such as exemptions from certain regulations). These principles are the yin and yang of religious liberty."[23]

Supporters of Charitable Choice, in contrast, argue that a congregation's right to maintain its "religious integrity" does not represent a violation of the First Amendment but instead reflects more fully the intent of the framers of the U.S. Constitution to create a federal government which is neutral toward religion. The supporters say they have a right to share their religious teachings with their clients as long as they do not use government funds for such purposes. Amy Sherman, a leading evangelical spokesperson who has worked for the Hudson Institute and as an advisor to George W. Bush, argues, "Religious groups must be able to refer to biblical principles" and "pray with program participants . . . while offering assistance."[24] She contends that it is only through "tough love" and "spiritual motivation" that social service providers will be able to exert "moral authority and cultivate traditional values among welfare recipients."[25] She is not alone. It has been reported that white evangelicals "see in welfare reform a chance for churches to lead nonbelievers to Christ as they deliver social services or help in the community."[26] Even Indianapolis Juvenile Judge James Payne believes that social service providers funded by government should be encouraged "to teach spiritual values.[27]

The constitutional issues raised by Charitable Choice demonstrate that this provision marks a significant departure from longstanding interpretations of the First Amendment. What is also new about Charitable Choice is that its proponents hope to fund not the larger religiously affiliated organizations such as Catholic Charities and the Salvation Army, which have a long history of providing services with federal money, but congregations, who have never before received public resources.

Indianapolis offers an excellent vantage point to examine the nation's growing support for faith-based organizations and Charitable Choice. Under Mayor Goldsmith, who began supporting faith-based programs before most national politicians did, Indianapolis has been heralded as an exemplar by those who promote the expansion of faith-based initiatives. Goldsmith has served President Bush as a "domestic advisor" and chair of the Corporation for National and Community Service. Finally, the rhetoric and debates about faith-based organizations in Indianapolis differ little from those that appear in national circles.

In 1999, during the presidential campaign, the idea of government support for religious congregations to provide social services received national attention. In Indianapolis, this proposal had gained popularity in the mid-1990s when Mayor Goldsmith reached out to churches as part of his response to social issues. Like other cities, Indianapolis in the mid-1990s suffered from rising crime and an influx of highly addictive drugs such as crack cocaine. In his search to identify the "stabilizing" institutions in inner-city neighborhoods, Goldsmith described how both local residents and urban planners directed him to churches.[28]

Congregations fit well into Goldsmith's larger privatization agenda. He believed that urban residents in Indianapolis suffered from a "crisis of citizenship."[29] One might expect that he, like so many social critics, was concerned about the tenuous links between citizens and government as expressed through citizen apathy and low voter turnout. Goldsmith, however, rarely talked about the rights of citizens to exercise political rights, and he openly questioned the usefulness of citizens trying to empower themselves by gaining direct political power. He criticized what he termed the "political activist version of empowerment," whereby citizens focus on "political power seeking." Instead he exalted a "Tocquevillian empowerment" in which citizens focus energy on the voluntary sector.[30]

For Goldsmith, citizenship was not about rights but responsibilities. He proclaimed that "citizenship cannot be achieved in the abstract or by a government agency bestowing rights on individuals." Instead, he proposed, citizenship is realized "by the responsibility people take for their neighborhoods," and he warned, "In hard-pressed city neighborhoods . . . citizenship does not come easily."[31] In short, Goldsmith's definition of citizenship was of a privatized citizenry, where one seeks to influence society primarily through the civil sphere, leaving the governance of the formal political apparatus to successful managers like himself.

This conceptualization of citizenship had a dramatic impact on the way Goldsmith understood urban maladies and their solutions. Rejecting the notion that social ills such as poverty and unwed motherhood have complex systemic causes, Goldsmith argued that the only way to address any urban ill was to first encourage individual responsibility. "Personal responsibility is not the only condition for overcoming social problems, but without it, all other attempts to eliminate the causes of poverty, crime, and civic apathy do little good."[32] Notably, during the prosperity of the 1990s, Goldsmith believed that individuals who did not prosper were responsible for their own failures. He never addressed the fact that wages for America's lowest paid workers, adjusted for inflation, had fallen by 40 percent in the last three decades of the twentieth century.[33]

In Goldsmith's view, an individual's irresponsibility often stemmed from a lack of morality and religious attachment. As a society, we must recognize that "problems such as high teen birth rates, infant mortality, poor educational performance, drug use and crime cannot be disconnected from emotional and spiritual needs."[34] Traditional public programs would never be able to solve such problems because "government can't teach values." Hope resided, Goldsmith assured his constituents, in "churches and community organizations."[35]

By conceptualizing social ills in religious and moral terms and ignoring structural impediments, Goldsmith had a justification to bypass traditional social service providers and look to churches. What, more specifically, did churches offer that traditional governmental and secular private social services could not? Churches, according to Goldsmith, "provide not only a service but a community of care and support."[36] More important, they sought to "transform" the individual rather than merely serve. "Social pathologies are best confronted not by large programs administered by professionals, but by citizens actively engaged in making their communities safer, healthier, more compassionate, and more productive."[37] The underprivileged who receive services from faith-based organizations were fortunate to experience "the truest sense of empowerment, because it is truly people of faith reaching inside that person and developing the power of the inner self."[38]

These assumptions grounded social policy in Indianapolis and across the nation. Franklin D. Raines, chairman and CEO of Fannie Mae, explained why "Faith-Based Charity Works": "We've seen that when it comes to alleviating poverty and social pathologies, the most creative force in America are volunteer organizations in those neighborhoods where it takes faith to believe transformation is possible."[39] Kirk Fordice, the former governor of Mississippi, put it more bluntly: "God, not government, will be the savior of welfare recipients."[40]

Goldsmith appealed not just to the spiritual values of individuals, but also to the public's anti-government sensibility when he diagnosed social problems in urban America and called on churches. He contrasted faith-based programs he initiated in Indianapolis to large government programs, such as the 1960s War on Poverty, which he claimed were responsible for "perpetuating the problems rather than helping to solve them."[41] "With high levels of government spending, social problems only worsened."[42] The problem, he diagnosed, was that "federal programs to relieve poverty have preyed on the lack of democratic capacity in urban neighborhoods."[43] They "suffocate local efforts, displace indigenous leadership, and reward bad behavior."[44] It would be best, according to Goldsmith, if "welfare as a social program" would "cease to exist."[45] Goldsmith promised, "By putting faith in our neighborhoods, we are jointly beginning a new chapter in the history of American citizenship."[46]

Ironically, many of the government programs Goldsmith assailed, such as the War on Poverty, actually employed small, community-based organizations. It was, in fact, during the War on Poverty that the federal government for the first time turned to nonprofit organizations to provide services, and under this system many religious charities, both large and small, thrived. Goldsmith also failed to acknowledge that programs such as Medicare and Medicaid—two of the largest government programs—provided health services to the poor who did not have access to private care. Finally, Goldsmith ignored the fact that nonprofits are less likely than public agencies to serve the most needy without restriction.[47]

Goldsmith not only denounced government programs. He expressed suspicion of large bureaucratic nonprofits that he believed resembled governmental agencies in form and function. He warned, for example, that "not all nonprofits are neighborhood-based, and many of them deal with the same issues as impersonal government agencies."[48] His animus toward large-scale nonprofits stemmed from their ostensible proximity to government and thus their success in winning government contracts. He complained that "[government] gives preference to large organizations that specialize in understanding government but are often less familiar with neighborhood dynamics."[49] Public authorities who favored such organizations, he contended, were making a mistake and should direct attention to small neighborhood and faith-based organizations that "have the detailed knowledge and flexibility necessary to administer the right combination of loving compassion and rigorous discipline appropriate for each citizen."[50] As mayor, Goldsmith "tended to focus on congregations new to community-service efforts, ignoring existing faith-based programs."[51]

As faith-based initiatives gained national popularity in the late 1990s, debates about them resembled those that had already taken place in Indianapolis. President Bush's Office of Faith-Based and Community Initiatives does not promote large-scale religious nonprofits that have received government money for decades. Instead the Office has focused on "improv[ing] government's relationship with small, front line faith and community organizations."[52] This orientation reflects Bush's belief that "some of our greatest welfare programs in America are on the street corners of inner-city America in a house of worship."[53] It is possible that Bush wants to limit government's support of large nonprofits because they have voiced concern about, or even outright opposition to, his faith-based initiative. In addition, larger nonprofits tend to be politically moderate, or in some cases liberal, and therefore not the constituency from whom Bush seeks support. In contrast, many of the congregations that Bush has reached out to tend to be theologically and politically conservative.

Although the public tends to look favorably on Bush's faith-based initiative—in one poll 75 percent expressed support for funding faith-based organizations—large-scale charities have expressed resentment that Bush and other faith-based proponents ignore the work they have been doing for decades.[54] In one op-ed piece, for example, Reverend Fred Krammer, the former head of Catholic Charities U.S.A., described how "one of the most frustrating aspects of the current debate is how it has effectively ignored how we and other religiously sponsored social service agencies have had such partnerships with government for more than a century."[55] Although those partnerships have involved hundreds of millions of dollars—in 1994 Catholic Charities received "65 percent of an almost $2 billion budget" from federal grants and contracts—faith-based proponents rarely mention these historic ties between religion and state.[56] Their silence is particularly glaring when one considers large cities such as Chicago, where in 2000 Catholic Charities received 77 percent of its support from government funds, Lutheran Social Services 70 percent, and the Jewish Federation of Metropolitan Chicago 22 percent.[57] When faith-based proponents do make reference to large-scale religious charities, it is more often than not to demonstrate the need for increased contact with small organizations. For example, after noting that Catholic Charities and the Salvation Army have a "good track record of using public dollars to carry out their efforts," Goldsmith ended with the caveat, "Yet there is something special about small community groups, whether secular or religious."[58]

What is it that makes them so special? According to Goldsmith, "they bring grassroots knowledge of their community and nearby residents to the social services equation." "Whatever they may lack in administrative capacity and specialization is often compensated by their proximity to the people they serve, their credibility in the neighborhood, and their sense of mission."[59] Policy makers want to deploy small, neighborhood-based religious organizations because they are ostensibly "in touch" with the neighborhood in a way large organizations could never be. Proponents insist that the men and women who work for small organizations are volunteers who care deeply for the people they serve and are more dedicated than professional social workers and counselors. Furthermore, same proponents claim that professional providers are by definition ill equipped. Indianapolis Juvenile Judge James Payne, in a decision to send children to churches and other religious groups, complained, "We have a problem. Our psychologists, our social workers, our probation officers, are not getting through. I am seeing the same kids come through. They are not listening to the warnings, the counseling, the therapy."[60]

Implicit in the argument that faith-based organizations are more in tune with their neighborhoods is the idea that they will have freedom to shape services according to local needs and cultures. Ironically, conservatives opposed the War on Poverty's community action agencies because they were given just that kind of freedom. At that time, however, politicians objected to the use of greater autonomy to promote political activism and critiques of government. When faith-based proponents today talk about giving nonprofits autonomy, they are hoping those organizations will respond to the personal needs of the underprivileged, not that they will develop advocacy roles. Advocating for greater autonomy and control has become a means to support devolution of services and legitimize the privatization of government services.

The shift toward faith-based solutions to urban ills has affected how policy makers understand accountability and efficacy. After leaving office, Goldsmith defended his privatization policies. He claimed services were more efficient in a privatized system because competition forced providers to be more accountable. In theory, a city contracts out services only to those who can prove their efficacy. Demanding high standards in 1994, Goldsmith threatened to cut off funds to Indianapolis's fourteen community centers that "operated without clear measures of program success."[61] One would have expected Goldsmith to apply the same standard to all organizations, and on the surface it seemed that he had. Like President Bush, Goldsmith frequently asserted that faith-based organizations merited support because they were "highly effective," more so than government agencies or secular nonprofits. "If our agencies would structure programs according to well-defined results, then the logical providers of program services would be the organizations that produce results. In many of our cities and communities, this means the smaller frontline organization such as the church or the community center."[62]

However, what Goldsmith meant by "well-defined results" was never clear. He criticized public social welfare programs in which government "regulators" "measure" success by "how many cases have been handled, how many people showed up for a training class, how many people successfully completed the program."[63] How else, one might wonder, can public authorities possibly measure success if not by counting the number of people who successfully completed a program? The answer for Goldsmith was clear: a social service program should aim for "transformed" lives. He lauded faith-based organizations precisely because they "measure their work not in terms of the people they serve or their cost-effectiveness, but in terms of lives transformed."[64] In order to make use of such organizations, Goldsmith warned that we would have to rethink government standards and rules that "plague efforts to work with effective organizations." The most troublesome rules, those that require "credentialing" of drug counselors and social workers, he claimed, "often discriminate against faith-based providers."[65] Judge Payne concurred. "Insistence on certain professional credentials raised the bar and lowered the quality of services received by juveniles."[66]

There was an obvious problem in consistency here. Goldsmith justified privatization by highlighting how it generated competition, fostered efficiency, increased effectiveness, and mandated accountability. However, regarding faith-based organizations, he not only supported a vague, indefinable measure of success—a "transformed life"—but he did not require accountability. At times he even dismissed the issue of cost-effectiveness.

Goldsmith's refusal to create and enforce standard measures of success follow from his anti-government and anti-regulatory views. According to Goldsmith, regulation strangles innovation and distracts organizations from their work. "Community organizations are far too busy with the pressing needs of their neighbors to translate and comply with these myriad rules."[67] Rejecting established measures of success, Goldsmith discredited the professional social workforce that provides those measures. Thus, he legitimized the position dear to evangelicals and conservatives that social problems are fundamentally individual sins cured by individual redemption.

An examination of Goldsmith's celebrated faith-based program, the Front Porch Alliance (FPA), demonstrates how he instituted his political philosophy. Goldsmith began his first term emboldened by the belief that neighborhoods "ought to figure out for themselves not only what they wanted but where and how to get it—including producing and procuring goods and services themselves."[68] When the FPA was created in 1997, Goldsmith hoped that Indianapolis's neighborhood residents would create alliances with each other and together strengthen their neighborhoods. He expected churches, with other community institutions, to join the FPA. As one commentator noted, however, the FPA attracted churches almost exclusively and became a de facto "steeple alliance."[69] But this identification of the FPA as a religious venture did not bother Goldsmith, who had always contended that "value-enhancing" institutions were uniquely situated to identify the needs of the underprivileged.

To facilitate the involvement of congregations, the FPA created a line of communication between the mayor's office and religious figures who had not previously had much contact with governmental authorities. Through the FPA, the mayor encouraged churches to provide social services, often in partnership with other institutions. For instance, churches in collaboration with the school system provided tutoring services and operated summer youth programs. To help stem the tide of crime, thirty churches embarked on an "Adopt-A-Block" program, through which church members maintained upkeep on city streets. A smaller group of churches formed a Ten Point Coalition, based on the model of Reverend Eugene Rivers in Boston, to communicate to drug dealers that honest citizens were taking their streets back. As evidence of the success, Goldsmith proclaimed that the FPA transformed a crime-ridden alley into a community garden.[70]

The FPA differed from many faith-based programs in other cities in that relatively little public money was channeled directly to churches. In 1997 the FPA employed only nine workers and its operating budget was $100,000.[71] In 1999, its budget increased to $400,000, still a small sum. The amount reserved for direct grants to churches was modest. In 1998 and 1999 combined, a total of only $129,000 was so dispersed, generally in sums less than $5,000.[72] However, the FPA did help congregations leverage funds from other sources, both private foundations and federal programs. City employees assisted churches in writing grant proposals. Goldsmith estimated that these efforts resulted in more than $750,000 for religious organizations.[73]

In any case, Goldsmith surely did not oppose channeling large sums of money directly to churches, but Indianapolis had neither the funds nor mandate to do so. The state, however, through the Charitable Choice provision of the 1996 welfare reform act, did have such power, and under Governor Frank O'Bannon, a Democrat, tried to expand the role congregations played in the delivery of TANF funded services by creating FaithWorks. FaithWorks, a part of Indiana's Department of Social Services, helps religious congregations write grant proposals and manage government funds. In addition, it has actively recruited religious organizations to offer social services. In regular meetings, it informs congregations of the resources available and encourages them to pursue those funds.

Through the FPA and FaithWorks, Indiana policy makers have pursued faith-based policies that mirror the Bush administration's national initiatives. The U.S. departments of Health and Human Services (HHS), Housing and Urban Development (HUD), Education, and Labor have all created programs to reach out to faith-based organizations that qualify for federal funds. HHS, for example, controls a $25 million "compassion fund" designed to "provide technical assistance to help faith-based and community organizations to effectively access funding sources, operate and manage their programs, develop and train staff, expand the reach of programs into the community, and replicate promising programs."[74] The Education Department, under Rod Paige, has been especially aggressive. It provides "writing workshops" for religious leaders to inform them about federally funded tutoring services they can apply for, and it helps them prepare proposals. In Oklahoma, Secretary Paige instructed educational authorities to "contact every minister in the state."[75] To shield these faith-based providers from competition with "slick" grant writers, the Education Department instituted a "novice applicant rule" that gives bonus points to "inexperienced bidders."[76]

Labor Secretary Elaine Chao announced in July 2002 that the Department of Labor planned to distribute more than $17 million to "link faith-based and grassroots community organizations to the nation's One-Stop Career System."[77] Most of the grants, Chao explained, would "help ministry groups provide job training and counseling to the needy."[78] Chao justified the grants by reiterating the president's understanding of the role religion plays in the lives of the underprivileged. "Faith-based and community organizations can be powerful catalysts in transforming people's lives."[79]

President Bush's belief that "in the final analysis, there is no overcoming anything without faith—be it drugs or alcohol or poverty or selfishness or flawed social policy" has had important implications for the operation of all federal departments.[80] In March 2002, when a HUD-funded homeless shelter in Sioux Falls, South Dakota, was criticized for requiring clients to pray before meals, HUD Secretary Mel Martinez defended the practices and policies of faith-based organizations that receive government money. Prayer, he asserted, was "integral to the success of the program." He claimed, furthermore, that any government attempt to "change the messages [faith-based organizations] deliver to clients . . . violates the Establishment clause of the Constitution, and it most certainly calls into question the service providers' right to free speech and the free exercise of religion."[81]

When asked about HUD's active recruitment of faith-based organizations, Martinez explained that he followed Bush's dictates: "One of the highest priorities of this administration is to improve the quality of our society's response to persons in need and there's no better way to do that than encouraging the participation of community and faith-based organizations." According to Martinez, the government sees faith-based organizations as central to the provision of basic services previously provided by government. "At a time of hardship in our cities, when government resources are already stretched to the limit, we need these guardian angels."[82]

Just as Charitable Choice provoked heated debate, these programs instituted by federal departments have generated conflict. Critics single out the "novice applicant" rule as an inappropriate form of affirmative action for religious groups. They highlight the irony that Bush, who refuses to endorse race-based affirmative action, justifies the novice applicant rule with arguments and principles similar to advocates of affirmative action. Bush and his colleagues claim, for example, that their sole goal is to provide a "level playing field" and that faith-based groups are entitled to special treatment because they have traditionally been "discriminated against."[83]

Other critics focus on the issue of accountability. Bush's domestic policy in general and his education policies in particular are premised on the principle of accountability. The "No Child Left Behind" act requires students and teachers to prove their proficiency and holds school administrators responsible for "failing" schools. However, when explaining why the federal government should fund faith-based organizations, Bush, like Goldsmith, talks about the ability of congregations to "change hearts" and "transform lives." He does not explain how such effects can be identified and measured.

Lastly, some express concern about how well congregations, most of which have little experience providing social services, will deal with the complex social problems facing the underprivileged. It is one thing to find a former welfare recipient a job, but an altogether harder task to provide social support, such as child care and transportation, that facilitates success in the workplace. Depression and drug addiction prohibit the move of some welfare recipients into the workforce. In contrast to public agencies, which have an obligation to serve all clients equitably, private agencies have traditionally been selective in choosing their clients and have focused on individuals whose problems are the easiest to solve. How will "novice" religious providers address protracted problems of depression and drug abuse?[84]

What does the case of Indianapolis, where faith-based programs predated but closely resembled federal initiatives, teach us? The experience of FaithWorks demonstrates that many churches support Bush's policies and express interest in federal programs, but very few actually bother to apply for funds. In a survey of Indiana churches, 52 percent said they would be interested in applying for federal funds. Among mainline Protestants, the figure was 69 percent.[85] However, very few churches attended the FaithWorks meetings to learn about and apply for funds. Of 9,000 congregations in Indiana, including 1,200 in Indianapolis, approximately 300 representatives attended the first four meetings sponsored by Faith-Works. Of the 300, only 10 percent received government contracts. Indianapolis congregations were awarded 25 percent of those contracts.[86] In recent years, the numbers have not increased. In 2001, fewer than 100 congregations attended FaithWorks seminars, and in 2002 only 122 attended.[87] Low response rates affected other faith-based programs in Indianapolis. When the FPA announced a competition for summer grants to provide services for children, only 70 congregations out of a total of 1,200 applied.[88] In a survey of congregations with ties to the FPA, 20 percent expressed frustration with their involvement with the city.[89]

Indiana is not the only state that has failed to recruit congregations who state in surveys that they are interested. When asked in a national survey if they would apply for federal funds, 36 percent of churches nationwide responded positively.[90] However, a study conducted by the Center for Public Justice, which looked at Charitable Choice initiatives in nine states including three of the nation's largest—California, Texas, and Illinois—found that "in the first three years after Charitable Choice took effect, it produced a total of only 84 new partnerships."[91]

What explains the disjuncture between congregational interest and actual involvement? Congregations often lack the capacity. Although many say they are interested in providing social services, few have any experience with the kinds of services the government will fund. Under TANF, the government can fund vocational training, counseling, drug treatment, child care, and after-school programs.[92] But few congregations offer those services. Less than 4 percent provide either child care or counseling, and little more than 1.5 percent offer job training. In fact, only 3 to 6 percent of programs congregations sponsor actually qualify for TANF funds.[93] Furthermore, while some church day care centers serve low-income children, many serve middle-class parishioners who pay fees.

Another problem congregations face is inadequate staffing to provide services. In Indianapolis, the median congregation has only 150 members.[94] The majority, 80 percent, have less than one worker devoting 25 percent of his or her time to social services.[95] In other words, most congregations have no staff person who devotes even 25 percent of his or her time to social services activity.[96] Furthermore, congregations on average spend little on social services. For congregations with 5,000 or more members, the annual average is $2,800. For congregations with 150 or fewer, the average is $975.[97]

While increased government funding might help congregations provide social services, no amount of funding can change one of the largest obstacles congregations face. Notwithstanding rhetoric to the contrary, most congregations do not know their neighborhoods very well. Sociologist Art Farnsley, in his exhaustive survey of churches in Indianapolis, concluded that congregations are not the local, neighborhood institutions policy makers imagine. Not only do many congregants live outside the neighborhood in which their church is located, the churches themselves are not integrated into their neighborhoods.[98] When congregations in Indianapolis in the late 1990s expressed interest in providing services, it quickly became clear that many were ignorant of existing programs run by other institutions in their communities. Understandably, the funds and special assistance congregations received from the mayor's office created "resentment among those organizations that have labored in service for years and decades" particularly when those funds were redirected from these experienced organizations to churches.[99] According to Lamont Hulse, director of the Indianapolis Neighborhood Resource Center, policy makers also "displayed great naiveté about existing neighborhoods, a lack of understanding about neighborhood realities and impatience with the deliberate pace by which communities, including neighborhood associations, operate."[100]

Many churches, it seems, are not "neighborhood institutions" keenly aware of local structures and problems. This helps explain why so few responded to the invitation of FaithWorks to learn about and apply for TANF funds, and it accounts for the limitations of the now defunct FPA. Although Mayor Goldsmith describes the program as a success in national forums, Indianapolis residents harbor mixed opinions. When asked to evaluate the success of the FPA, Hulse commented that it was "something of a moving target, so it's difficult to say whether it succeeded" even "by its own terms." In describing FPA's goals, Hulse commented, "There was implicit in FPA the notion that churches would bring clients in touch with a higher power and that would solve their problems." He wondered, "should government be giving money for this purpose?"[101] Susan Williams, a former Democratic city councilperson, has pointed out how, in a city with scarce resources, Goldsmith's policies "pitted the churches against the neighborhood associations against the community development groups for the same dollars."[102]

The FPA's short three-year life suggests an absence of support within the city to sustain it. Many of the FPA's ostensible successes proved fleeting. The revitalized alleyway Goldsmith has mentioned frequently, evidence that faith communities can save urban America, has not been maintained. In 2000, the small 200-square-yard alleyway had "trash litter[ing] the ground" and few signs of life besides "some distressed-looking trees and a few dying plants of flowers."[103]

In public pronouncements, both Bush and Goldsmith express unmitigated confidence in the ability of churches to save urban America. Why, then, have not congregations responded to the call for service? Some do not have the means; others lack interest. The primary problem is simple. According to sociologist Art Farnsley, "the average, ordinary congregation has its hands full just meeting the worship and religious education needs of its members."[104]

Scholars, politicians, and policy makers have debated the merits and drawbacks of government funding for faith-based programs, both in terms of efficacy and in terms of constitutional issues. One of the most striking features of the debates has been the minimal attention paid to the poor themselves. Scholarly observers of Charitable Choice rarely discuss how the 1996 welfare reform act, of which it is a part, places strict time limits on the poor who receive such services. Under TANF, welfare recipients are restricted to two years of consecutive support and five years of lifetime support. The time frame for "transforming" the individual is short.

While it would be helpful to gather data about the lives of the poor in order to assess the efficacy of this social welfare policy, we unfortunately have little information about former welfare recipients because politicians have refused to fund studies. On more than one occasion, the U.S. Congress has voted against a "tracking" bill that would have provided hard data about the poor leaving the welfare rolls. For many politicians the fact that welfare rolls declined was sufficient proof of the success of welfare reform. In the words of now deceased Senator Paul Wellstone of Minnesota, who submitted the tracking bill, we went from "welfare as we 'know it' to welfare as we do not know it."[105]

Despite the refusal of the federal government to study the effects of welfare reform, individual states, including Indiana, have conducted their own studies. Indiana began implementing welfare reform in 1995 and was required by federal law to provide data about its impact. (It is ironic that the federal government required the states to monitor the effects of state-initiated welfare reform programs but has chosen not to study the impact of its own legislation.) Indiana's study revealed that although the welfare rolls declined by more than 50 percent between 1994 and 1999, the financial state of the poor was still precarious. Less than one-half of former recipients still held jobs two years after leaving the rolls. Those who left for employment earned an average of $4,334 and received $2,429 in TANF payments and Food Stamps.[106] More than 40 percent of the women cited "lack of adequate child care" as an impediment to employment.[107] Modest state subsidies for child care are woefully inadequate to meet the existing needs. According to one 1999 estimate, the state would have to double its appropriations for child care to meet the need of all qualifying parents.[108]

National studies by groups like Network, a Catholic social justice lobby, have found similar results around the country. In 1999, Network, frustrated because the government was "unable for the most part to tell us what is happening to people after they leave the welfare rolls," conducted an extensive survey of former welfare recipients in Michigan, New York, Pennsylvania, Ohio, Illinois, Florida, Texas, and California. Recognizing that "those hardest hit are hardest to find," Network interviewed not only those persons with phones and permanent residences, but also those seeking assistance at homeless shelters and food banks. In "Poverty Amid Plenty: The Unfinished Business of Welfare Reform," Network reported "a sharp rise in the 'disconnected' people without either jobs or government assistance.[109] Network found that even among full-time workers, 24 percent "cannot provide sufficient food for their children." Furthermore, more than 1.25 million people had lost access to Medicaid because of increased income.[110] With the downturn in the economy since 2001, the numbers seeking assistance have begun to increase. In Indiana the welfare rolls rose from 30,000 in 1999 to 52,000 in 2002.[111]

Considering the widely held assumption that faith-based organizations are supposed to have the ability to alleviate poverty and solve many other social ills, one might conclude that faith communities have failed. In fact, the main reason why the poor are not doing well has very little to do with what churches *do* or *do not do*. Notwithstanding recent political rhetoric, churches are not at the center of the nation's social welfare system. Instead, public social welfare agencies, secular nonprofits, and for-profits provide the bulk of services.

The most striking feature of recent social welfare policy is the new role played by for-profit firms. In 2001, 27 percent of all TANF contracts nationwide were awarded to for-profit firms, compared to only 7 percent to faith-based organizations.[112] In many states, for-profit companies are the primary providers for the poor and needy. In the late 1990s, Maximus, a for-profit firm, received more than $350 million in government contracts, including a $4 million contract from Colorado and a $46 million contract from Wisconsin, to provide "job training and other services to welfare recipients."[113]

One reason states are attracted to for-profit firms is because policy makers hold work-first philosophies. The primary goal of a welfare system with a work-first philosophy is to get poor people employed, regardless of low pay or limited opportunity for advancement, and not to provide training or education. When Indiana first implemented welfare reform in 1995, it adopted a work-first strategy. In Indianapolis, Goldsmith aggressively pursued this strategy by hiring for-profit companies such as AmericaWorks. Reflecting on work-first policies, Goldsmith stated, "The best way to serve people was not through extensive training but by getting them into work and letting the employer train them."[114] Ironically, Goldsmith believed that churches should deliver social services because they ostensibly were grassroots institutions aware of local needs. But welfare services are often provided by nationally based for-profit companies with no ties to the neighborhoods they serve or even to any one state or city. Even more troubling, some for-profit firms have been accused of "inadequate and poor provision of services" and "misappropriation of funds."[115]

Consider the example of Virginia-based Maximus, Inc., one of the nation's leading for-profit firms engaged in welfare reform. Maximus has received hundreds of millions of dollars in contracts from public authorities in more than two dozen states. It has also been accused of serious mismanagement. In 1998, the state of Connecticut hired Maximus to oversee the payment of publicly funded child care. Speaking on behalf of the Connecticut State Employees Association, Rick Melita charged, "They [Maximus] underbid, overpromised, and they didn't deliver."[116] In Wisconsin, where Maximus has received more than $100 million in government contracts since 1997, the company has been plagued by scandal. The *Milwaukee Journal Sentinel* reported that the Legislative Audit Bureau "found nearly $800,000 in questionable spending by Maximus."[117] Linda Garcia, a nonprofit worker who has had close contact with Maximus's clients, alleges, "The standards of accountability and monitoring have been practically nonexistent. We're not seeing decent services provided to the community or a decrease in poverty or homelessness." She also contends that Maximus channels women into "low-paying jobs in order to quickly receive the bonus staff gets for placements."[118] These problems prompted fifty Milwaukee-area churches to join forces with state lawmakers and demand the cancellation of a $46 million contract that Maximus had been awarded.[119]

The work-first strategy, despite its appeal to conservatives, has not fared well in Indianapolis or elsewhere. Women leaving the rolls have poor employment records and tend to earn salaries insufficient to meet even their most basic needs.[120] Recognizing that former welfare recipients need more than a job, fifteen of the twenty states that had adopted work-first strategies in the 1990s abandoned that policy. Indiana is one of five states that remain committed to work-first.

Private charities in Indianapolis can confirm that the working poor continue to struggle. In the late 1990s, a time of celebrated national prosperity, Catholic Charities of Indianapolis witnessed the number of people attending its emergency crisis center double. Most who sought help were employed, in some cases with two jobs. The St. Vincent de Paul Society also saw working people in search of food rise significantly. Nationwide food banks have reported increases in employed persons and many families requesting assistance. One researcher has estimated that nationwide 50 percent of those seeking help from food programs are two-parent working-class families.[121] The fact that the poor who are fully employed must seek aid from private charities raises questions about welfare reform when success is measured solely by the decline in the rolls and the number of persons employed.

The case of Indianapolis reveals the limited goals of welfare reform in a city where social policy is based on the principles of privatization. It highlights how privatization, contrary to the claims of its proponents, has not led to greater citizen involvement and empowerment. Instead, according to Sheila Suess Kennedy, privatization has "minimized the contacts citizens have with their government" and encouraged "'experts' rather than citizens to guide public policy or policies." "While privatization is almost always defended as a method for producing smaller and more responsive government, in fact it simply empowers—*authorizes*—private interests to act under government's imprimatur, shifting the locus but not the magnitude of the task at hand."[122]

When the U.S. Congress abolished AFDC in 1996, a New Deal legacy came to an end. Leslie Lenkowsky, a supporter of Bush's faith-based initiatives, has astutely observed that "what is distinctive about the President's plan is not its reliance on proxies to provide the federal government's social services—this, as not a few conservatives have observed, was an innovation of the Great Society. What is distinctive, rather, is its unabashedly moral tone. That tone is a throwback to an era when the nation's charities were concerned not just with the material circumstances of those they helped but about their character and behavior as well."[123] Marvin Olasky, a former communist turned evangelical Christian, has captured and articulated this frame of mind. Olasky has influenced how conservatives, including President Bush, understand social policy.

Olasky's *The Tragedy of American Compassion* received little attention from the general public or academics when it was published in 1992. Olasky argues that immorality is the primary cause of most social ills, and that the United States did a better job caring for the poor in the late nineteenth century when private agencies and churches assumed a prominent role in their care. They succeeded, Olasky asserts, because they "stressed man's sinfulness, which only God's grace could change."[124] Historians who reviewed the book dismissed it as "romantic," "shallow," and, because of its gross historical inaccuracies, "bizarre"; the work of an ideologue.[125] Although academics dismissed Olasky's work, conservative politicians embraced it. U.S. Representative Newt Gingrich, among others, was sympathetic to Olasky's reading of the past and its implications for social policy. As Speaker of the House, Gingrich gave all freshman Republican congresspersons copies of the book.[126] Olasky's work also made a strong impression on fellow Texan George W. Bush. Olasky recalls how Governor Bush called to "discuss the policy implications of my findings"[127] and tried to model his policies in Texas on Olasky's ideas. In 1995, when the Texas Commission on Alcohol and Drug Abuse attempted to revoke the license of a Teen Challenge program—an explicitly Christian organization—because it refused to hire any professionally trained staff members, Bush rushed to the group's defense. He relaxed standards of "oversight and licensing" for the Teen Challenge Center because he believed its workers had "proven their effectiveness."[128] Bush's support for Teen Challenge reflected his conviction that "America will be changed one soul at a time."[129]

During his presidential campaign, Bush made "compassionate conservatism," a phrase coined by Olasky, a central theme, and he publicly acknowledged that "he [Olasky] has been one of the people who has been most helpful."[130] After Bush and Democratic candidate Al Gore announced they would both seek the aid of faith-based organizations to combat social ills, social welfare reformers who wished to increase the role of the private sector and of churches hailed states like Texas and Indiana that had never before been viewed as leaders in domestic policy.

Olasky has since come out against Bush's faith-based initiative because he believes government has no role to play in the provision of social services. Nevertheless, his ideas have helped provide the groundwork for faith-based programs in Indianapolis and nationwide. Goldsmith has commented that he wished he had written *The Tragedy of American Compassion*.

In the 1930s, when the nation confronted its worst economic depression, the federal government instituted the New Deal. Debate about the American welfare state ever since has centered around the relative merits of government assistance or private charity. Advocates of a "Tocquevillian" America have argued that private charities are best able to assist the underprivileged and that government is incapable of serving the poor. Public agencies, wedded to bureaucracies and indifferent to the emotional and spiritual needs of the poor, will always fail to address the true causes of poverty. The welfare state, this line of reasoning continues, has the further drawback of squeezing out the vibrant voluntary sector.

Supporters of America's welfare state have rarely articulated a clear philosophy. A select few have argued that our definition of citizenship should include social as well as political rights, but most supporters of public assistance offer pragmatic reasons to justify government assistance. They argue that the state has a responsibility to provide social services because the private sector is incapable of serving the nation's underprivileged. Without a convincing public philosophy, provision for the poor remains a form of public charity rather than an entitlement or a right of citizenship.

Missing from debates about the public and private sectors is attention to their interdependence. As the case of Indianapolis demonstrates, the relationship between government agencies and private charities, rarely one of competition, has generally been cooperative. In the 1930s, to keep expenditures low and bureaucracy small, the public sector looked to the private sector, and in the case of Catholic Charities the government provided important subsidies. In the 1940s and 1950s, the public lost interest in social welfare policy. When the plight of the poor became a national issue in the 1960s, however, government once again looked to the private sector to expand the welfare state. The War on Poverty channeled significant funds to nonprofit agencies. Even after the federal government dismantled War on Poverty programs, it continued to provide significant resources to the nonprofit sector. Political scientists credit the explosion in the number of nonprofits in the 1960s and 1970s to that public funding.

In the 1990s and in the twenty-first century, support for public provision has declined, and local, state, and federal governments are shifting responsibility for the needy to the private sector, both the nonprofit and for-profit arms. In the 1990s, a time of national prosperity, it was difficult for many Americans to imagine that anything other than personal factors—irresponsibility, immorality—caused social ills. Religious congregations seemed well positioned to provide social services because they promised to shape the moral values of those they served. Today, government is eager to redirect public resources from public agencies to the private sector, most notably religious organizations.

This policy raises fundamental questions about the nature of citizenship in a democratic society and sheds light on the longer history of social welfare. In contrast to most European nations, where social welfare has been defined as a right of citizenship, the U.S. has never embraced the notion that citizenship should include social obligations. Not only have many basic services for the underprivileged been left in the hands of the private sector, but even public provision has been precarious, easily withdrawn when the nation's political winds shift. Private social welfare organizations that have depended on public funding have found themselves especially vulnerable because most Americans view the services they provide as a charitable endeavor rather than a public responsibility. We would be remiss not to note, however, that the greatest cost is borne by the poor who continue to struggle to provide food and shelter for their families.

NOTES

Introduction

1. Catholic Charities of the Diocese of Indianapolis, "Handbook" (n.d.), Archives of the Archdiocese of Indianapolis, Indiana (Hereafter referred to as AAI).
2. Stephen Goldsmith, *Putting Faith in Neighborhoods: Making Cities Work through Grassroots Citizenship* (Indianapolis: Hudson Institute, 2002), 6.
3. For general books on the history of social welfare, see Michael B. Katz, *In the Shadow of the Poorhouse: A Social History of Welfare In America*, rev. ed. (New York: Basic Books, 1996); James T. Patterson, *America's Struggle against Poverty, 1900–1980* (Cambridge, Mass.: Harvard University Press, 1981); Edward Berkowitz and Kim McQuaid, *Creating the Welfare State: The Political Economy of Twentieth Century Reform* (Lawrence: University Press of Kansas, 1992); and William I. Trattner, *From Poor Law to Welfare State: A History of Social Welfare in America* (New York: Free Press, 1979). On social welfare since the War on Poverty, see Michael B. Katz, *The Undeserving Poor: From the War on Poverty to the War on Welfare* (New York: Pantheon, 1989).
4. Books specializing on race and/or gender include Linda Gordon, *"Pitied but Not Entitled": Single Mothers and the History of Welfare* (New York: Free Press, 1994); Linda Gordon, ed., *Women, the State, and Welfare* (Madison: University of Wisconsin Press, 1990); Robyn Muncy, *Creating a Female Dominion in American Reform* (New York: Oxford University Press, 1991); Seth Koven and Sonya Michel, eds., *Mothers of a New World: Maternalist Politics and the Origins of the Welfare State* (New York: Routledge, 1993); Gwendolyn Mink, *The Wages of Motherhood: Inequality in the Welfare State, 1917–1942* (Ithaca, N.Y.: Cornell University Press, 1995); and Jill Quadagno, *The Color of Welfare: How Racism Undermined the War on Poverty* (New York: Oxford University Press, 1994).
5. Katz, *In the Shadow of the Poorhouse*, x.
6. Theda Skocpol, "The Tocqueville Problem: Civic Engagement in American Democracy," *Social Science History* 21 (Winter 1997): 469. Also see Theda Skocpol and Morris P. Fiorina, eds., *Civic Engagement and American Democracy* (Washington, D.C.: Brookings Institution Press, 1999); and Jacob S. Hacker, *The Divided Welfare State: The Battle Over Public and Private Social Benefits in the United States* (Cambridge: Cambridge University Press, 2002).
7. On the issue of "contracting out," see Steven Rathgeb Smith and Michael Lipsky, *Nonprofits for Hire: The Welfare State in the Age of Contracting* (Cambridge, Mass.: Harvard University Press, 1993); Ralph M. Kramer, *Voluntary Agencies in the Welfare State* (Berkeley: University of California Press, 1981); Lester Salamon, *Partners in Public Service: Government-Nonprofit Relations in the Modern Welfare State* (Baltimore, Md.: Johns Hopkins University Press, 1995);

and Walter W. Powell and Elisabeth Clemens, eds., *Private Action and Public Good* (New Haven, Conn.: Yale University Press, 1998).

8. See Arthur Farnsley II, *Rising Expectations: Urban Congregations, Welfare Reform, and Civic Life* (Bloomington: Indiana University Press, 2003); Ram Cnaan with Robert Weinberg and Stephanie Brodie, *The Newer Deal: Social Work and Religion in Partnership* (New York: Columbia University Press, 2000); and Robert Wineburg, *A Limited Partnership: The Politics of Religion, Welfare and Social Service* (New York: Columbia University Press, 2000).

9. Farnsley, *Rising Expectations*, 21.

10. David J. Bodenhamer and Robert G. Barrows, eds., *The Encyclopedia of Indianapolis* (Bloomington: Indiana University Press, 1994), 53.

11. Ibid., 56.

12. Ibid., 1554.

1. Catholic Charities and the Making of the Welfare State

1. Weltha Kelly, "Survey of Catholic Charities Bureau of Indianapolis" (1935), Archives of the Archdiocese of Indianapolis, (AAI).

2. "Volunteer Activity," *Public Welfare in Indiana* 48 (March 1938): 10.

3. Historians have, of course, discussed in great depth the difficulties voluntary associations faced in meeting the needs of their members. For example, see Lizabeth Cohen, *Making a New Deal: Industrial Workers in Chicago, 1919–1939* (New York: Cambridge University Press, 1990); and Beth Wenger, *New York Jews and the Great Depression: Uncertain Promise* (New Haven, Conn.: Yale University Press, 1996).

4. On the New Deal in the South, see Douglas S. Smith, *The New Deal in the Urban South* (Baton Rouge: Louisiana State University Press, 1988); and Roger Biles, *The South and the New Deal* (Lexington: University Press of Kentucky, 1994). For a discussion of race and social welfare in the latter decades of the twentieth century, see Jill Quadagno, *The Color of Welfare: How Racism Undermined the War on Poverty* (New York: Oxford University Press, 1994).

5. For an excellent discussion of Catholic Charities on the national level, see Dorothy Brown and Elizabeth McKeown, *The Poor Belong to Us: Catholic Charities and American Welfare* (Cambridge, Mass.: Harvard University Press, 1998), 9.

6. U.S. Bureau of the Census, *Census of Religious Bodies*, 1936.

7. For a discussion of Catholic influence in Chicago, see Edward R. Kantowicz, "Cardinal Mundelein of Chicago and the Shaping of Twentieth Century American Catholicism," *Journal of American History* 68 (June 1981): 52–68.

8. Laurence J. Moore, *Citizen Klansmen: The Ku Klux Klan in Indiana, 1921–1928* (Chapel Hill: University of North Carolina Press, 1991).

9. Kelly, "Survey of Catholic Charities."

10. "Minutes of the Indianapolis Council of Social Agencies," 4 April 1932, Archives of the United Way of Indianapolis (AUWI).

11. On Catholics and the New Deal, see David J. O'Brien, *American Catholics and Social Reform: The New Deal Years* (New York: Oxford University Press, 1968); George Q. Flynn, *American Catholics and the Roosevelt Presidency, 1932–*

1936 (Lexington: University of Kentucky Press, 1968); and Evelyn Sterne, "Bringing Religion into Working-Class History," *Social Science History* 24 (Spring 2000): 149–182.

12. Community Fund of Indianapolis, "How 70,230 Citizens Saved a City" (1933), AUWI.

13. *Indianapolis Times,* 3 December 1934.

14. Ibid.; Catholic Charities of the Diocese of Indianapolis, "Handbook" (n.d.), AAI.

15. For a discussion of the city's Employment Work Committee, see Brad Sample, "To Do No Small Good: Philanthropy in Indianapolis, 1929–1933" (M.A. thesis, Indiana University–Purdue University Indianapolis, 1998).

16. Emma A. Winslow, *Trends in Different Types of Public and Private Relief in Urban Areas, 1929–1935* (Washington, D.C.: U.S. Government Printing Office, 1937), 104.

17. *Indiana Bulletin of Charities and Correction,* June 1933, 169.

18. "Minutes of the Meeting of the Indianapolis Council of Social Agencies," 22 May 1933, AUWI.

19. William C. Keane, "The Diocesan Directors of Catholic Charities," *Proceedings of the Seventeenth National Conference of Catholic Charities* (1931): 255–256.

20. Catholic Charities Bureau of the Diocese of Indianapolis, *Annual Report,* 1937.

21. Ibid.

22. *Indiana Catholic and Record,* 27 April 1934.

23. For works on Catholics and the New Deal, see note 11.

24. *Indiana Catholic and Record,* 9 February 1934.

25. Thomas R. Greene, "The Catholic Conference on Industrial Problems in Normalcy and Depression," *Catholic Historical Review* 77 (April 1991): 437–469.

26. John A Ryan, Address at the Regional Meeting of the Catholic Conference on Industrial Problems, Box 36, National Catholic Welfare Conference Records, Archives of the Catholic University of America (ACUA).

27. Community Fund of Indianapolis, "You've Asked the Questions" (1938), AUWI.

28. F. M. Vreeland, "The New Horizon in Social Work," *Indiana Welfare and News* 52 (October 1937): 4.

29. For a discussion of Jewish social workers responding to the expanding welfare state, see Wenger, *New York Jews and the Great Depression.*

30. Daniel J. Walkowitz, *Working with Class: Social Workers and the Politics of Middle Class Identity* (Chapel Hill: University of North Carolina Press, 1999): 141.

31. Catholic Charities Bureau of the Diocese of Indianapolis, *Annual Report,* 1937.

32. Ibid.

33. Ibid.

34. On privately employed social workers, see Walkowitz, *Working with Class,* 141–176.

35. John W. Mohr and Francesca Guerra-Pearson, "The Effect of State Intervention in the Nonprofit Sector: The Case of the New Deal," *Nonprofit and Voluntary Sector Quarterly* 25 (December 1996): 525–539.

36. Reverend August Fussenegger to Reverend John O'Grady, 23 March 1937, Folder: August Fussenegger, National Conference of Catholic Charities Collection, ACUA.

37. Edward M. Farrell, "Report on Meetings of Diocesan Directors of Catholic Charities," *Proceedings of the Twenty-Second National Conference of Catholic Charities* (1936): 249.

38. Catholic Charities Bureau of the Diocese of Indianapolis, *Annual Report*, 1939.

39. See Brown and McKeown, *The Poor Belong to Us*, 13–50. For a specific discussion of Indiana's "suitable home" clause, see "Assistance to Dependent Children is Now Being Given," *Indiana Welfare News*, November 1936, 4–5.

40. Katharine F. Lenroot, "Child Welfare and Social Reconstruction," *Proceedings of the Twenty-First National Conference of Catholic Charities* (1935): 36.

41. John J. Butler, "Presidential Address," *Proceedings of the Twenty-Second National Conference of Catholic Charities* (1936): 21.

42. Joseph LeBlond, "Catholic Charities and Governmental Programs of Child Care," *Proceedings of the Twenty-Fourth National Conference of Catholic Charities* (1938): 42.

43. Fussenegger to the Director of Catholic Social Services of Peoria, 5 November 1948, Fussenegger Papers, AAI.

44. See Brown and McKeown, *The Poor Belong to Us*.

45. Catholic Charities Bureau of the Diocese of Indianapolis, *Annual Report*, 1936; Catholic Charities Bureau of the Diocese of Indianapolis, *Annual Report*, 1939.

46. Catholic Charities Bureau of the Diocese of Indianapolis, *Annual Report*, 1939.

47. Catholic Charities, "Handbook" (n.d.), AAI.

48. Michael J. Doyle, "Practices Employed in the Working Relationship between Catholic Agencies and Public Departments" *Proceedings of the Twenty-Fifth National Conference of Catholic Charities* (1939): 103.

49. Council of Social Agencies of Indianapolis, "News Bulletin of the Council of Social Agencies" (May 1942); Research Department of the Indianapolis Council of Social Agencies, "Marion County Direct Relief Study, 1939–1943" (1943).

50. Research Department of the Indianapolis Council of Social Agencies, "Marion County Direct Relief Study, 1939–1943" (1943).

51. "Community Welfare Plan Saves Tax Dollars," *Public Welfare in Indiana*, January 1939, 12; Joanne Goodwin, *Gender and the Politics of Welfare Reform: Mothers' Pensions in Chicago, 1911–1929* (Chicago: University of Chicago Press, 1997).

52. "Community Welfare Plan Saves Tax Dollars," 12.

53. "Minutes of the Child Welfare Committee," 24 April 1939, AUWI.

54. *Indianapolis Star*, 1 January 1940. A discussion of Indianapolis's Trustee

2. A City of Families

1. Family Service Association of Indianapolis, *Annual Report*, 1957.
2. *Indianapolis Star*, 7 October 1938.
3. Elaine Tyler May, *Homeward Bound: American Families in the Cold War Era* (New York: Basic Books, 1988), 13. On women and the 1950s, see also Joanne Meyerowitz, "Beyond the Feminine Mystique: A Reassessment of Popular Mass Culture, 1946–1958," *Journal of American History* 79 (March 1993): 1455–1482; Eugenia Kaledin, *Mothers and More: American Women in the 1950s* (Boston: Twayne Publishers, 1983); Mary Jetzer, *The Dark Ages: Life in the United States, 1945–1960* (Boston: South End Press, 1982); William O'Neill, *American High: The Years of Confidence, 1945–60* (New York: Free Press, 1986); Leila J. Rupp and Verta Taylor, *Survival in the Doldrums: The American Women's Rights Movement, 1945 to the 1960s* (New York: Oxford University Press, 1987); and William Henry Chafe, *The American Woman: Her Changing Social, Political, and Economic Roles, 1920–1970* (New York: Oxford University Press, 1972).
4. For a discussion of the United Service Organization, see Gretchen Knapp, "Experimental Social Policymaking during World War II: The United Service Organizations (USO) and American War-Community Services (AWCS)," *Journal of Policy History* 12 (Spring 2000): 321–338.
5. Daniel T. Sheen, "The National Catholic Community Service Program," *Catholic Charities Review*, March 1941, 83.
6. Letta Irwin Shonle, "The Impact of the War on Group Work Agencies in Indianapolis" (M.A. thesis, Indiana University, 1944).
7. Susan Myers-Shirk, "'To Be Fully Human': U.S. Protestant Psychotherapeutic Culture and the Subversion of the Domestic Ideal," *Journal of Women's History* 12 (Spring 2000): 115.
8. Jeffrey M. Burns, *American Catholics and the Family Crisis, 1930–1962* (New York: Garland Publishing, 1988), 121.
9. Indianapolis Community Fund, pamphlet (1941), Archives of the United Way of Indianapolis (AUWI).
10. Indianapolis Community Fund, "25th Anniversary Report" (1944), AUWI.
11. Family Welfare Society of Indianapolis, *Annual Report*, 1945.
12. Indianapolis Community Fund, "These Are the Facts," n.d., AUWI.
13. Indianapolis Community Fund, "25th Anniversary Report" (1944), AUWI.
14. Indianapolis Community Fund, "These Are the Facts."
15. Patricia Bellard, "A Study of Social and Economic Status of a Selected Group of Applicants in Cases Active with the Family Service Association of Indianapolis, August 31, 1949" (M.A. thesis, Indiana University, 1951): 3.
16. Ibid.
17. Catholic Charities of the Diocese of Indianapolis, "Handbook" (n.d.), Archives of the Diocese of Indianapolis (AAI).

18. Catholic Charities Bureau of the Diocese of Indianapolis, *Annual Report*, 1942.

19. Marcel Kovarsky, "Current Purposes and Goals of Jewish Family Agencies," *The Jewish Social Service Quarterly* 30 (Spring 1954): 282–288.

20. Milfred Arnold, *Child Welfare at the Crossroads* (U.S. Children's Bureau), Publication no. 327, 1949.

21. Burns, *American Catholics*, 114.

22. May, *Homeward Bound*, 7.

23. Burns, *American Catholics*, 120.

24. Peter Berger, "The Second Children's Crusade: Overemphasis on the Family in Suburbia's Churches Is Basically Subversive of the Christian Mission," *The Christian Century*, December 2, 1959, 1399–1400.

25. Family Service Association of Indianapolis, *Handbook for Members* (Indianapolis: Family Service Association of Indianapolis, 1952), 80.

26. Daniel J. Walkowitz, *Working with Class: Social Workers and the Politics of Middle-Class Identity* (Chapel Hill: University of North Carolina Press, 1999), 201.

27. Ruby Little, "History of the Family Service Association of Indianapolis, Indiana, 1835–1950" (M.A. thesis, University of Chicago, 1951), 123.

28. Family Welfare Society, *Annual Report*, 1945.

29. Shonle, "The Impact of the War," 81.

30. *Indianapolis Star*, 1 January 1956.

31. Catholic Charities Bureau of the Diocese of Indianapolis, *Annual Report*, 1948.

32. Kovarsky, "Current Purposes and Goals of Jewish Family Agencies," 287.

33. Burns, *American Catholics*, 100.

34. Quoted in Burns, *American Catholics*, 251.

35. *Family Life Clinic: Report of the Study Committee* (Indianapolis: Church Federation of Indianapolis, 1958).

36. Ibid.

37. Little, "History of the Family Service Association," 121.

38. Family Service Association of Indianapolis, *Handbook for Members*, 73.

39. Catholic Charities Bureau of the Diocese of Indianapolis, *Annual Report*, 1948.

40. Ibid.

41. *Indianapolis Star*, 1 January 1956.

42. *Indianapolis News*, 25 March 1949.

43. Catholic Charities Bureau of the Diocese of Indianapolis, *Annual Report*, 1948.

44. Kovarsky, "Current Purposes and Goals of Jewish Family Agencies," 283.

45. Ibid., 281.

46. Burns, *American Catholics*, 222, 264.

47. Ibid., 224.

48. For an excellent discussion of the pastoral counseling movement, see Myers-Shirk, "To Be Fully Human."

49. Family Service Association of Indianapolis, *Handbook for Members*, 60–61; *Indianapolis Times*, 2 September 1951.

50. George Thorman," Marriage Counseling and Social Casework" (M.A. thesis, Indiana University, 1951), 7.

51. *Indianapolis Star*, 24 February 1952.

52. Florence Hollis, *Women in Marital Conflict: A Casework Study* (New York: Family Service Association of New York, 1949), 86.

53. Thorman, "Marriage Counseling and Social Casework," 8.

54. Ibid., 8.

55. Hollis, *Women in Marital Conflict*, 221.

56. Burns, *American Catholics*, 215.

57. Walter Imbiorski, ed., "The Pre-Cana Conference," *New Cana Manual* 79, cited in Burns, *American Catholics*, 227.

58. Catholic Charities Bureau of the Diocese of Indianapolis, *Annual Report*, 1948.

59. *Indianapolis News*, 16 October 1947.

60. Marcella Lucille DeVoe et al., "Homemaking Service in the Family Service Association of Indianapolis, January 1, 1952–December 31, 1952" (M.A. thesis, Indiana University, 1953), 20.

61. Ibid., 32.

62. Ibid., 53.

63. Ibid., 45.

64. Ibid., 15.

65. Ibid., 10.

66. Ibid., 45.

67. Little, "History of the Family Service Association," 127.

68. DeVoe, "Homemaking Services," 13.

69. Ibid.

70. Lillian Cahn, "A Study of 61 Families Receiving Aid to Dependent Children in Behalf of One Eligible Child, Marion County Department of Public Welfare" (M.A. thesis, Indiana University, 1951), 28.

71. Evelyn Dunbar, "The Employment Experience of Thirty-Five White Mothers Receiving Aid to Dependent Children in Marion County and Its Effects on Their Families during the War and the Post-war Period" (M.A. thesis, Indiana University, 1949), 42.

72. Ibid., 43.

73. Ibid.

74. Naomi J. Thomas, "The Employment Experience of Forty Negro Mothers Receiving Aid to Dependent Children in Marion County and Its Effects on Their Families during the War and Post-war Period" (M.A. thesis, Indiana University, 1948), 29.

75. Dunbar, "The Employment Experience," 45–46.

76. *Indianapolis News*, 22 February 1952.

77. *Indianapolis Star*, 25 September 1961.

78. *Indianapolis Star*, 20 January 1956.

79. *Indianapolis Star*, 10 October 1955.

80. Catholic Charities Bureau of the Diocese of Indianapolis, *Annual Report*, 1956.

81. Walkowitz, *Working with Class*, 204.

82. Richard A. Cloward and Irwin Epstein, "Private Social Welfare's Disengagement from the Poor: The Case of Family Adjustment Agencies," in George A. Brager and Francis P. Purcell, eds., *Community Action against Poverty: Readings From the Mobilization Experience* (New Haven, Conn.: College and University Press, 1967), 50–51.

83. Myra L. Brenneman et al., "Brief Service Cases in the Family Service Association of Indianapolis, January 1, 1952–June 30, 1952" (M.A. thesis, Indiana University, 1953), 24–26.

84. Doris Harpole Hosmer, "Evaluation of Case Results: A Study of the Evaluation Process in 100 Service Only Cases in the Family Welfare Society of Indianapolis" (M.A. thesis, Indiana University, 1942).

85. Brenneman, "Brief Service Cases," 110.

86. Ibid.

87. Ibid.

88. Jacqueline Berns, "A Study of a Selected Group of Patients Served by Marion County Children's Guidance Committee" (M.A. thesis, Indiana University, 1958), 77.

89. Ibid., 66–77.

90. Henry S. Mahs, "Sociocultural Factors in Psychiatric Clinic Services for Children," *Smith College Studies in Social Work* 25 (February 1955): 6. Quoted in Cloward and Epstein, "Private Social Welfare's Disengagement from the Poor," 41.

91. Dorothy Fahs Beck, *Patterns in the Use of Family Service Agencies* (New York: FSA of America, 1962), 26, 31.

92. Cloward and Epstein, "Private Social Welfare's Disengagement from the Poor," 48.

93. Weltha Kelly, "Survey of the Catholic Charities Bureau of Indianapolis" (1935), Catholic Charities Bureau of the Diocese of Indianapolis.

94. Agencies Caring for Unwed Mothers, Child Welfare Committee, 17 January 1938, AUWI.

95. Betty Ann Adney, "A Study of Case Records of 108 Babies Born to Patients of Suemma Coleman Home in Selected Years 1910 to 1946" (M.A. thesis, Indiana University, 1947), 52.

96. Rickie Solinger, *Wake Up Little Susie: Single Pregnancy and Race before Roe v. Wade* (New York: Routledge, 1992). For another excellent work on unwed mothers, see Regina Kunzel, *Fallen Women, Problem Girls: Unmarried Mothers and the Professionalization of Social Work, 1890–1945* (New Haven, Conn.: Yale University Press, 1993).

97. *Indianapolis Star*, 10 October 1955.

98. *Indianapolis News*, 24 February 1961.

99. *Indianapolis Times*, 12 May 1955.

100. *Indianapolis News*, 21 February 1961.

101. *Indianapolis Times*, 11 May 1955.

102. *Indianapolis Times*, 11 May 1955.

103. Adney, "A Study of Case Records," 22.
104. *Indianapolis Star,* 10 May 1955.
105. *Indianapolis News,* 23 February 1961.
106. *Indianapolis Times,* 13 May 1955.
107. *Indianapolis Times,* 13 May 1955.
108. *Indianapolis News,* 23 February 1961.
109. Adney, "A Study of Case Records," 54.
110. *Indianapolis News,* 23 February 1961.
111. Ibid.
112. *Indianapolis Star,* 10 October 1955.
113. Church Federation of Indianapolis, "Federation News: An Annual Report," 1949.
114. Catholic Charities Bureau of the Diocese of Indianapolis, *Annual Report,* 1952.
115. *Indianapolis Star,* 10 February 1952.
116. Ibid.
117. *Indianapolis News,* 15 August 1959.
118. Community Surveys Inc., "Child Welfare Needs and Services in Indianapolis and Marion County," August 1947, 22.
119. Ah Nee Leong, "The Application Process as Reflected in 53 Aid to Dependent Children Cases Approved by the Marion County Department of Public Welfare, July–December, 1948" (M.A. thesis, Indiana University, 1950), 17, 40–41.
120. Gordon Lionel Jacobs, "Non-participation in the Food Stamp Plan: A Study of Reasons for Non-participation in the Food Stamp Plan of Fifty Whites and Fifty Negro Aid to Dependent Children Recipients Living in Center Township, Marion County, Indiana" (M.A. thesis, Indiana University, 1942), 1.
121. Leong, "The Application Process," 80.
122. Acts of Indiana, 1945, ch. 69, sec. 1
123. Leong, "The Application Process," 79–80.

3. Rediscovering Poverty, Redefining Community

1. *Indianapolis* Recorder, 10 July 1965; *Indianapolis Star,* July 2, 1965.
2. Classic studies of the War on Poverty include Frances Fox Piven and Richard A. Cloward, *Regulating the Poor: The Functions of Public Welfare* (New York: Pantheon Books, 1971); and Daniel P. Moynihan, *Maximum Feasible Misunderstanding: Community Action in the War on Poverty* (New York: Free Press, 1969). More recent histories include Michael Katz, *The Undeserving Poor: From the War on Poverty to the War on Welfare* (New York: Pantheon, 1989); Jill Quadagno, *The Color of Welfare: How Racism Undermined the War on Poverty* (New York: Oxford University Press, 1994); and Nancy A. Naples, *Grassroots Warriors: Activist Mothering, Community Work, and the War on Poverty* (New York: Routledge, 1998).
3. U.S. Census Report, Indiana, 1960.
4. Ibid.
5. For a discussion of housing in Indianapolis, see Richard Pierce, "Be-

neath the Surface: African-American Community Life in Indianapolis, 1945–1970" (Ph.D. dissertation, Indiana University, 1996).

6. Ibid., 194.

7. Ibid., 133–175.

8. The relationship between the War on Poverty and the civil rights movement has been one of the most debated issues, with Frances Fox Piven and Richard A. Cloward arguing in *Regulating the Poor* that the War on Poverty was designed, in part, to respond to urban black discontent. Other scholars argue that the War on Poverty was originally designed to reach white Appalachians and that only later did its focus turn to urban blacks. For example, see Katz, *The Undeserving Poor.*

9. The literature on civil rights leaders and organizations is considerable. For examples, see David J. Garrow, *Bearing the Cross: Martin Luther King, Jr. and the Southern Christian Leadership Conference* (New York: Morrow Press, 1986); Adam Fairclough, "The Preachers and the People: The Origins and Early Years of the Southern Christian Leadership Conference, 1955–1959," *The Journal of Southern History* 52 (August 1986): 403–440; and William M. King, "The Reemerging Revolutionary Consciousness of the Reverend Dr. Martin Luther King, Jr., 1965–1968," *The Journal of Negro History* 71 (Winter 1986): 1–22.

10. For an example of a book that highlights the connections between all three in various cities, see Ralph M. Kramer, *Participation of the Poor: Comparative Community Case Studies in the War on Poverty* (Englewood, N.J.: Prentice-Hall, 1969).

11. *Indianapolis Times*, 1 April 1965.

12. For a discussion of Daley and the War on Poverty, see Quadagno, *The Color of Welfare*, 52–59.

13. *Indianapolis Star*, 4 April 1965.

14. Ibid.

15. Christian Inner City Association pamphlet, 8 December 1965. Folder 35, Box 127, Indianapolis Urban League Papers (IULP), Indiana Historical Society.

16. Ibid.

17. Christian Inner City Association, "Statement on Anti-Poverty Program," 17 July 1965, Folder 35, Box 127, IULP.

18. "Archdiocesan and Diocesan Programs under Equal Opportunity Act through June 30, 1967," Folder—National Catholic Coordinating Committee, Box 174, Collection #76, Archives of the Catholic University of America (ACUA).

19. *Philadelphia Gazette*, 10 January 1967.

20. "Archdiocesan and Diocesan Programs under Equal Opportunity Act through June 30, 1967," Folder—National Catholic Coordinating Committee, Box 174, Collection #76, ACUA.

21. For an excellent discussion of the War on Poverty in Mississippi, see Quadango, *The Color of Welfare.*

22. *Indianapolis Times*, 1 April 1965.

23. *Indianapolis Recorder*, 10 April 1965.

24. *Indianapolis Recorder*, 4 April 1965.

25. *Indianapolis Recorder*, 10 April 1965.

26. Ibid.
27. *Indianapolis Times*, 4 April 1965.
28. *Indianapolis Recorder*, 24 April 1965.
29. *Indianapolis Recorder*, 6 July 1965.
30. *Indianapolis Star*, 17 May 1967.
31. *Indianapolis Recorder*, 17 July 1965.
32. Interreligious Committee Against Poverty (ICCA), "Testifying on the Equal Opportunity Amendments of 1967 (HR 8311)," Collection #76, ACUA.
33. *Indianapolis Star*, 4 April 1965.
34. *Indianapolis Times*, 11 April 1965.
35. *Indianapolis Star*, 4 April 1965.
36. *Indianapolis Times*, 4 April 1965.
37. Christian Inner City Association, Pamphlet, July 1965, Folder 35, Box 127, IULP.
38. *Indianapolis Times*, 11 April 1965.
39. Ibid.
40. *Indianapolis Times*, 22 April 1965.
41. Ibid.
42. *Indianapolis Times*, 13 May 1965.
43. Indianapolis Field Report, Community Action Against Poverty, Folder—Indianapolis Record Group 381, National Archives (NA).
44. Katz, *The Undeserving Poor*, 100.
45. U.S. Census Report, Indiana, 1960.
46. *Indianapolis Star*, 21 January 1968.
47. *Indianapolis Recorder*, 25 December 1965.
48. Sign-Off Check List, Office of Inspection, Folder—1965–1966, Record Group 381, NA.
49. *Indianapolis Star*, 22 December 1965.
50. *Indianapolis Star*, 30 September 1970.
51. Indianapolis and Administration, 29 April 1966, Folder—Indianapolis, 1965–66, NA.
52. For a discussion of the Welfare Rights Organization, see Naples, *Grassroots Warriors;* and Anne M. Valk, "'Mother Power': The Movement for Welfare Rights in Washington D.C., 1966–1972," *Journal of Women's History* 11 (2000): 34–58.
53. *Indianapolis Times*, 13 July 1958.
54. Official Report of the Indiana Welfare Investigation Committee (1944), 5–7.
55. Ibid., 7, 29.
56. It needs to be pointed out that even those white widowed women who received ADC often had difficulty making ends meet on their meager public assistance and many were forced to seek other sources of support, including employment. For a general discussion of the creation of ADC, see Linda Gordon, *Pitied but Not Entitled: Single Mothers and the History of Welfare, 1890–1935* (New York: The Free Press, 1994).
57. *Indianapolis Times*, 29 November 1961.
58. *Indianapolis Times*, 22 February 1961.

59. *Indianapolis Star*, 22 September 1961.
60. Catholic Social Services, 1966 Agency Evaluation. AAI.
61. *Indianapolis Times*, 5 August 1961.
62. *Criterion*, 14 January 1972.
63. Ibid.
64. Catholic Social Services, 1966 Agency Evaluation. AAI.
65. *Indianapolis News*, 22 September 1967
66. *Indianapolis Star*, 22 June 1967.
67. John Daum to Ted Jarvis, memo, Indianapolis Sign-Off, n.d., Folder—Indianapolis, 1965–1966, Record Groups 381, NA.
68. *Indianapolis Recorder*, 7 May 1966.
69. *Indianapolis Star*, 14 April 1966.
70. *Indianapolis Star*, 17 August 1967.
71. *Indianapolis Recorder*, 30 March 1968.
72. Ibid.
73. *Indianapolis News*, 7 December 1965.
74. Ibid.
75. *Indianapolis Recorder*, 30 March 1968.
76. *Indianapolis Star*, 26 November 1967.
77. *Indianapolis Recorder*, 4 November 1967.
78. *Indianapolis Star*, 26 November 1967.
79. *Indianapolis Recorder*, 4 November 1967.
80. Ibid.
81. Ibid.
82. Ibid.
83. Ibid.
84. Ibid.
85. *Indianapolis Star*, 13 August 1967.
86. *Indianapolis Recorder*, 24 February 1968.
87. *Indianapolis Star*, 13 August 1967.
88. *Indianapolis Recorder*, 9 March 1968.
89. *Indianapolis Recorder*, 3 August 1968.
90. *Indianapolis Star*, 7 May 1968.
91. *Indianapolis News*, 27 October 1969.
92. *Indianapolis News*, 21 November 1968.
93. *Indianapolis Star*, 13 September 1970.
94. *Indianapolis News*, 27 October 1969.
95. *Indianapolis Star*, 13 September 1970
96. Ibid.
97. *Indianapolis Star*, 13 August 1967.

4. "Beyond Religious Boundaries"

1. *Indianapolis News*, 4 October 1972.
2. The most impressive and innovative historical work on white flight has been done by Thomas J. Sugrue in *The Origins of the Urban Crisis: Race and Inequality in Postwar Detroit* (Princeton, N.J.: Princeton University Press, 1996).

3. See Etan Diamond, *Souls of the City: Religion and the Search for Community in Postwar America* (Bloomington: Indiana University Press, 2003).

4. Ibid., 115.

5. *Indianapolis Times,* 7 November 1964.

6. Diamond, *Souls of the City,* chapter 2.

7. See John McGreevy, *Parish Boundaries: The Catholic Encounter with Race in the Twentieth-Century Urban North* (Chicago: University of Chicago Press, 1996); and Gerald Gamm, *Urban Exodus: Why the Jews Left Boston and the Catholics Stayed* (Cambridge, Mass.: Harvard University Press, 1999).

8. *Indianapolis Times,* 25 July 1961.

9. See Steven Rathgeb Smith and Michael Lipsky, *Nonprofits for Hire: The Welfare State in the Age of Contracting* (Cambridge, Mass.: Harvard University Press, 1993); Lester Salamon, *Partners in Public Service: Government-Nonprofit Relations in the Modern Welfare State* (Baltimore, Md.: Johns Hopkins University Press, 1995); and Walter W. Powell and Elisabeth Clemens, eds., *Private Action and Public Good* (New Haven, Conn.: Yale University Press, 1998).

10. Diamond, *Souls of the City,* 96.

11. Patricia Mooney Melvin, "Changing Contexts: Neighborhood Definition and Urban Organization," *American Quarterly* 37 (1985): 357–367.

12. Community Service Council of Metropolitan Indianapolis, "South-Central Area Analysis" (Indianapolis, 1961).

13. Indianapolis Council of Social Agencies, "Leisure Time Services: Indianapolis near Northeast Area" (1947).

14. For a discussion of urban ministries, see Clifford Green, ed., *Churches, Cities, and Human Community: Urban Ministry in the United States, 1945–1985* (Grand Rapids, Mich.: Wm. B. Eerdmans, 1996).

15. "Inner City Task Force" (1963), Folder 7, Box 42. The Church Federation of Greater Indianapolis, Indiana Historical Society (CFGI).

16. Minutes, Inner City Task Force, 3 December 1965, Folder 9, Box 42, CFGI.

17. Ibid.

18. Edwin Becker, *From Sovereign to Servant: The Church Federation of Greater Indianapolis* (Indianapolis: Church Federation of Greater Indianapolis, 1987), 99.

19. Ibid., 106.

20. "Agenda Elements," Inner City Task Force (11 January 1966), Folder 9, Box 42, CFGI.

21. Ibid.

22. Ibid.

23. "A Review of Some Questions," 24 September 1968, Folder 12, Box 42, CFGI.

24. Minutes, Inner City Unit, 27 December 1966, Folder 9, Box 42, CFGI.

25. Jason Lantzer, "Tradition, Transition, Turmoil, and Triumph: Indianapolis Episcopalians Confront the 1960s and 1970s" (M.A. thesis, Indiana University, 1999), 12.

26. Norman Faramelli, Edward Rodman, and Anne Scheibner, "Seeking to

Hear and to Heed in the Cities: Urban Ministry in the Postwar Episcopal Church," in Green, ed., *Churches, Cities, and Human Community*, 104–105.

27. *Indianapolis Star,* 30 April 1960.
28. *Indianapolis News,* 27 January 1969.
29. Faramelli, Rodman, and Scheibner, "Seeking to Hear and Heed," 119.
30. *Indianapolis News,* 19 February 1966.
31. Becker, *From Sovereign to Servant,* 132.
32. "Indianapolis—FPCC" (1965), Methodist Church Records, DePauw University.
33. *Indianapolis News,* 8 May 1964.
34. *Together/News Edition* (April 1964).
35. "Indianapolis—FPCC" (1965), Methodist Church Records, DePauw University.
36. *Indianapolis Star,* 22 August 1971.
37. "Indianapolis—FPCC" (1965), Methodist Church Records, DePauw University.
38. *Indianapolis Star,* 22 August 1971.
39. Community Service Council of Metropolitan Indianapolis, "North-Central Section Area Analysis" (Indianapolis, 1961).
40. "A Study of Mayer Chapel Neighborhood Services, Community Service Council," May 1962, AUWI.
41. "A Study of Catholic Social Services and St. Elizabeth's Home," National Conference of Catholic Charities (1966), AAI.
42. *Indianapolis Star,* 30 January 1970.
43. Ibid.
44. Jeffrey K. Hadden, *The Gathering Storm in the Churches* (New York: Doubleday & Co., 1969).
45. *Indianapolis News,* 25 May 1967.
46. *Indianapolis News,* 24 June 1965.
47. *Indianapolis News,* 3 October 1972.
48. Ibid.
49. For works on religion in the city during the nineteenth and early twentieth centuries, see Carol Smith Rosenberg, *Religion and the Rise of the American City: The New York City Mission Movement, 1812–1870* (Ithaca, N.Y.: Cornell University Press, 1971); Mary Mapes, "Visions of a Christian City: The Politics of Religion and Gender in Chicago's City Missions and Protestant Settlement Houses" (Ph.D. dissertation, Michigan State University, 1998); and Diane Winston, *Red Hot and Righteous: The Urban Religion of the Salvation Army* (Cambridge, Mass.: Harvard University Press, 1999).
50. "Staff Report on Christamore House," April 1961, Community Service Council of Indianapolis.
51. Ibid.
52. *Indianapolis News,* 5 October 1972.
53. Luther E. Smith, Jr., "To Be Untrammeled and Free: The Urban Ministry Work of the CME Church: 1944–1990," in Green, ed., *Churches, Cities, and Human Community,* 71.
54. George D. Younger, "'Not by Might, nor by Power': Urban Ministry

in American Baptist Churches," in Green ed., *Churches, Cities, and Human Community*, 50.

55. "Presidents of Regional Ministerial Associations" (1957–1958), Folder 14, Box 102. CFGI.
56. *Indianapolis Star*, 30 November 1968.
57. *Indianapolis Star*, 15 April 1972.
58. "Response to Inner City Needs," 26 November 1968, Folder 9, Box 42, CFGI.
59. Ibid.
60. Adolph Hansen to Reverend Landrum E. Shields, Folder 8, Box 102, CFGI.
61. See Becker, *From Sovereign to Servant*, 109; and Diamond, *Souls of the City*, 131–132.
62. Community Service Council of Indianapolis, "Inner-City" (1961).
63. *Indianapolis Star*, 26 January 1969.
64. *Indianapolis Star*, 22 November 1969.
65. Becker, *From Sovereign to Servant*, 79.
66. Ibid., 104.
67. Ibid.
68. Smith and Lipsky, *Nonprofits for Hire*, 55.
69. *Indianapolis Star*, 26 January 1969.
70. "The Church Federation and Indianapolis Housing Problems," 20 April 1967, folder 1, Box 80, CFGI.
71. "Inner City Unit: Background Material," Folder 9, Box 42, CFGI.
72. "Executive Director's Report to Board of Directors," 5 August 1970, Folder 4, Box 80, CFGI.
73. "Report to the Annual Meeting," 20 January 1969, Folder 1, Box 80, CFGI.
74. "Annual Meeting, 1969," 23 February 1970, Folder 5, Box 80, CFGI.
75. "Executive Director's Report to Board of Directors," 5 August 1970, Folder 4, Box 80, CFGI.
76. Untitled, 14 May 1971, Folder, Box 80, CFGI.
77. "Report to Annual Meeting," 20 January 1969, Folder 1, Box 80, CFGI.
78. "Annual Report, 1969," 23 February 1970, Folder 5, Box 80, CFGI.
79. "Proposal for the Renewal of an Inner-City Neighborhood," 19 July 1971, Folder 9, Box 80, CFGI.
80. "Listing of Organizations Developing Housing Programs for Indianapolis Metropolitan Region," June 1969, Folder 3, Box 80, CFGI.
81. "Report to Annual Meeting," 20 January 1969, Folder 2, Box 80, CFGI.
82. *Indianapolis Star*, 26 January 1969.
83. "Report to Annual Meeting," 20 January 1969, Folder 2, Box 80, CFGI.
84. "Inner City Unit: Background Material," Folder 9, Box 42, CFGI.
85. Catholic Social Services of Indianapolis, "Child Welfare Evaluation," 1979, AAI.
86. National Conference of Catholic Charities, "A Study of Catholic Social Services and St. Elizabeth's Home," (1966).

87. Neighborhood Community Service Program, *Annual Report*, September–December 1973, AAI.
88. Catholic Social Services of Indianapolis, *Annual Report*, 1979, AAI.
89. Neighborhood Community Service Program, *Annual Report*, September–December 1973, AAI.
90. Catholic Social Services of Indianapolis, *Annual Report*, 1980, AAI.
91. *Indianapolis Star*, 16 February 1971.
92. *Indianapolis Star*, 13 January 1970.
93. *Indianapolis Star*, 10 September 1972.
94. Dr. Lucille Hecker to Board of Directors of HOME, 23 June 1972, Folder 8, Box 80, CFGI.
95. George Maley to Development Committee of HOME, untitled memo ("HOME Memo"), 5 August 1972, Folder 8, Box 80, CFGI.
96. "Proposal for the Renewal of an Inner City Neighborhood," 19 July 1971, Folder 9, Box 80, CFGI.
97. *Indianapolis Star*, 7 December 1972.
98. "HOME Memo."
99. Ibid.
100. Smith and Lipsky, *Nonprofits for Hire*, 62–63.
101. Ibid., 208.
102. Green, *Churches, Cities, and Human Community*, 20.

5. "One Soul at a Time"

1. Stephen Goldsmith, *Putting Faith in Neighborhoods: Making Cities Work through Grassroots Citizenship* (Indianapolis: Hudson Institute, 2002).
2. Stephen Goldsmith, quoted in Arthur Farnsley II, *Rising Expectations: Urban Congregations, Welfare Reform, and Civic Life* (Bloomington: Indiana University Press, 2003), 69.
3. Eyal Press, "Lead Us Not into Temptation," *The American Prospect* 12 (9 April 2001).
4. *Indianapolis Star*, 29 January 2001.
5. George W. Bush, quoted in Byron R. Johnson, "Assessing the Effectiveness of Faith-Based Organizations: A Review of the Literature," transcript of the 2003 Annual Research Conference Breakfast Session, the Roundtable on Religion and Social Welfare Policy. Center of Religious Research and Urban Civil Society, http://www.religionandsocialpolicy.org.
6. *New York Times*, 12 April 2002.
7. For a discussion of the 1996 welfare reform act that places it within a broader historical context, see Gwendolyn Mink, *Welfare's End* (Ithaca, N.Y.: Cornell University Press, 2002).
8. Initially the program was called Aid to Dependent Children (ADC), but its name was later changed to Aid to Families with Dependent Children (AFDC). For the sake of consistency and clarity, this chapter uses the more recent name even when referring to the program in its early years.
9. Sharon Daly, "Welfare: A Catholic Response," *Church* (Winter 1997), 21.
10. Excellent monographs on the New Deal include Michael B. Katz, *In the*

Shadow of the Poorhouse: A Social History of Welfare in America (New York: Basic Books, 1986); James T. Patterson, *America's Struggle against Poverty, 1900–1994* (Cambridge, Mass.: Harvard University Press, 1999); Gwendolyn Mink, *The Wages of Motherhood: Inequality in the Welfare State, 1917–1942* (Ithaca, N.Y.: Cornell University Press, 1995); Linda Gordon, *Women, the State, and Welfare* (Madison: University of Wisconsin Press, 1991); and Linda Gordon, *Pitied but Not Entitled: Single Mothers and the History of Welfare* (New York: Free Press, 1994).

11. For a discussion of race and welfare, see Jill Quadagno, *The Color of Welfare: How Racism Undermined the War on Poverty* (New York: Oxford University Press, 1994).

12. On the issue of single mothers, see Rickie Solinger, *Wake Up Little Susie: Single Pregnancy and Race before Roe v. Wade* (New York: Routledge, 1992); and Regina Kunzel, *Fallen Women, Problem Girls: Unmarried Mothers and the Professionalization of Social Work, 1890–1945* (New Haven, Conn.: Yale University Press, 1993).

13. Thomas Harvey, "Government Promotion of Faith-Based Solutions to Social Problems: Partisan or Prophetic?" *Nonprofit Sector Research Fund*, The Aspen Institute Working Paper Series (July 1997).

14. For an excellent discussion of privatization in Indianapolis, see Ingrid Ritchie and Sheila Suess Kennedy, eds., *To Market, To Market: Reinventing Indianapolis* (New York: University Press of America, 2001).

15. On the issue of "contracting out," see Steven Rathgeb Smith and Michael Lipsky, *Nonprofits for Hire: The Welfare State in the Age of Contracting* (Cambridge, Mass.: Harvard University Press, 1993); Ralph M. Kramer, *Voluntary Agencies in the Welfare State* (Berkeley: University of California Press, 1981); Lester Salamon, *Partners in Public Service: Government-Nonprofit Relations in the Modern Welfare State* (Baltimore, Md.: Johns Hopkins University Press, 1995); and Walter W. Powell and Elisabeth S. Clemens, *Private Action and the Public Good* (New Haven, Conn.: Yale University Press, 1988).

16. Ellen Dannin, "To Market, to Market: Caveat Emptor," in Ritchie and Kennedy, eds., *To Market, to Market*, 11.

17. Stephen Goldsmith, quoted in Sheila Suess Kennedy, "Governing a City: Thirty-Two Years," in Ritchie and Kennedy, eds., *To Market, to Market*, 75.

18. Ibid., 71.

19. Stephen Goldsmith, quoted in Jack Miller, "Privatization in Indianapolis: Problems, 'Proximity Issues,' and Oscar Robertson Smoot," in Ritchie and Kennedy, eds., *To Market, to Market*, 350.

20. Dannin, "To Market, To Market: Caveat Emptor," 11.

21. Stephen Monsma, *When Sacred and Secular Mix: Religious Nonprofit Organizations and Public Money* (Lanham, Md.: Rowman & Littlefield, 1996).

22. Doug Brown and Jeanie Stokes, "Losing Faith: Turf Battles Derail Funding," *The Nonprofit Sector Times*, 1 February 2002.

23. Melissa Rogers, "Should We Put Faith in Charitable Choice?" *The Responsive Community* (Fall 2000).

24. Amy Sherman, quoted in Press, "Lead Us Not into Temptation."

25. Ibid.

26. Farnsley, *Rising Expectations*, 189.
27. Ibid., 90.
28. Goldsmith, *Putting Faith in Neighborhoods*, 112.
29. Ibid., 3.
30. Ibid., 227–229.
31. Ibid., 18.
32. Ibid., 11.
33. Eric Schlosser, *Fast Food Nation: The Dark Side of the All-American Meal* (New York: Houghton-Mifflin, 2001), 10.
34. Goldsmith, *Putting Faith in Neighborhoods*, 75.
35. Ibid., 112.
36. Ibid., 113.
37. Ibid., x.
38. Ibid., 119.
39. F. D. Raines, "Faith-Based Charity Works," *Commentary* 15 (February 2001).
40. Press, "Lead Us Not into Temptation."
41. Goldsmith, *Putting Faith in Neighborhoods*, 44.
42. Ibid., 6.
43. Ibid., 50.
44. Ibid., 6.
45. Ibid., 73.
46. Ibid., xi.
47. *New York Times*, 24 April 2001.
48. Goldsmith, *Putting Faith in Neighborhoods*, 75.
49. Ibid., 90.
50. Ibid., 8.
51. Lamont J. Hulse, "Empowering Neighborhoods," in Ritchie and Kennedy, eds., *To Market, to Market*, 220.
52. Goldsmith, *Putting Faith in Neighborhoods*, 109.
53. *New York Times*, 12 April 2002.
54. Reuters, 10 April 2001.
55. Thomas Harvey, "Government Promotion of Faith-Based Solutions."
56. Dorothy Brown and Elizabeth McKeown, *The Poor Belong to Us: Catholic Charities and American Welfare* (Cambridge, Mass.: Harvard University Press, 1998), 194.
57. *Chicago Tribune*, 1 February 2001.
58. Goldsmith, *Putting Faith in Neighborhoods*, 109–112.
59. Ibid.
60. James Payne, quoted in Goldsmith, *Putting Faith in Neighborhoods*, 116.
61. Hulse, "Empowering Neighborhoods," 215.
62. Goldsmith, *Putting Faith in Neighborhoods*, 93.
63. Ibid., 77.
64. Ibid.
65. Ibid., 124.
66. Farnsley, *Rising Expectations*, 31.
67. Goldsmith, *Putting Faith in Neighborhoods*, 91.

68. William Blomquist, "Organizational Change as a Management Tool: Mayor Goldsmith's Approach," in Ritchie and Kennedy, eds., *To Market, to Market*, 89.

69. Robert Cole, "Fresh Currents: The Front Porch Alliance," *Religion and Community: A Newsletter of the Project on Religion and Urban Culture* 4, no. 5 (Fall 2000): 5.

70. Goldsmith, *Putting Faith in Neighborhoods*, 16 and 79.

71. Lamont Hulse, quoted in Cole, "Fresh Currents," 5.

72. Hulse, "Empowering Neighborhoods," 220.

73. Goldsmith, *Putting Faith in Neighborhoods*, 81.

74. Department of Health and Human Services, "HHS Announces Availability of Funds to Assist Faith-Based and Community Organizations," press release, 19 June 2002.

75. *Boston Globe*, 21 July 2002.

76. Ibid.

77. U.S. Newswire, 1 July 2002.

78. *Washington Times*, 18 April 2002.

79. U.S. Newswire, 1 July 2002.

80. *The New Republic* 4, no. 493 (26 February 2001).

81. HUD statement, "Martinez Seeks to End Faith-Based Discrimination in HUD Programs," 15 March 2002.

82. Ibid.

83. Ibid.

84. Smith and Lipsky, *Nonprofits for Hire*, 133.

85. The Polis Center, "Indiana Congregations' Human Services Program: A Report of a Statewide Survey," 1 February 2001, 3–5.

86. Ted Slutz, "Congregations and Charitable Choice," *Religion and Community: A Newsletter of the Project on Religion and Urban Culture* 4, no. 5 (Fall 2000): 2.

87. Sheila Suess Kennedy and Wolfgang Bielefeld, eds., "Charitable Choice: Results from Three States—Interim Report on the Implementation of Charitable Choice in Three States," Center for Urban Policy and the Environment, Indiana University, 47.

88. Farnsley, *Rising Expectations*, 43.

89. Hulse, "Empowering Neighborhoods," 222.

90. Mark Chavez et al., "The National Congregations Study: Background, Methods, and Selected Results," *Journal for the Scientific Study of Religion* 38 (1999): 458–476.

91. Slutz, "Congregations and Charitable Choice," 2.

92. Indiana Family and Social Services Administration, "FaithWorks Indiana: Indiana's Initiative to Support Faith-Based Organizations in Providing Services to Hoosier Families in Needs," (Indiana Family and Social Services Administration, 2000).

93. The Polis Center, "Indiana Congregations' Human Services Program," 11.

94. Farnsley, *Rising Expectations*, 36.

95. Ibid., 55.

96. Polis Center, "Indiana Congregations' Human Services Program," 7.

97. Ibid., 11.
98. Farnsley, *Rising Expectations*.
99. Hulse, "Empowering Neighborhoods," 221.
100. Lamont J. Hulse, "Targeting Neighborhoods," in Ritchie and Kennedy, eds., *To Market, to Market*, 195.
101. Cole, "Fresh Currents," 5.
102. *The Post-Tribune*, Gary, Indiana, 30 January 2001.
103. Cole, "Fresh Currents," 5.
104. Farnsley, *Rising Expectations*, 70–71.
105. Paul Wellstone, "America's Disappeared," *The Nation* 269 (12 July 1999).
106. David J. Fein et al., "The Indiana Welfare Reform Evaluation: Program Implementation and Economic Impacts after Two Years," November 1998, Prepared for Division of Family and Children, Family and Social Services Administration, by Abt. Associates Inc. and the Urban Institute.
107. Ibid., xv.
108. Jim Hmurovich, comments made at the Indiana Catholic Conference: Partnering for Self-Sufficiency, 28 September 1999.
109. "Poverty Amid Plenty: The Unfinished Business of Welfare Reform," *Network: A National Catholic Social Justice Lobby* (1999).
110. *Washington Post*, 24 July 1999.
111. Kennedy and Bielefeld, eds., "Charitable Choice: Results from Three States," 50.
112. General Accounting Office (GAO), "Welfare Reform: Interim Report on Potential Ways to Strengthen Federal Oversight of State and Local Contracting," http://www.gao.gov/new.items/d02245.pdf.
113. Bill Berkowitz, "Prospecting among the Poor: Welfare Privatization," Applied Research Center, 2001.
114. Goldsmith, *Putting Faith in Neighborhoods*, 57.
115. Berkowitz, "Prospecting among the Poor," 6.
116. Rick Melita, quoted in Berkowitz, "Prospecting among the Poor," 7.
117. Berkowitz, "Prospecting among the Poor," 8.
118. Linda Garcia, quoted in Berkowitz, "Prospecting among the Poor," 9.
119. Berkowitz, "Prospecting among the Poor," 8.
120. *Chicago Tribune*, 30 September 2003.
121. *The Washington Post*, 24 July 1999.
122. Sheila Suess Kennedy, "Accountability: The Achilles Heel," in Ritchie and Kennedy, eds., *To Market, to Market*, 142–145.
123. Leslie Lenkowsky, "Funding the Faithful: Why Bush Is Right," *Commentary Magazine* 111, no. 6 (June 2001).
124. Press, "Lead Us Not into Temptation."
125. David Grann, "Where W. Got Compassion," *The New York Times Magazine*, 12 September 1999.
126. Ibid.
127. Press, "Lead Us Not into Temptation."
128. Ibid.
129. *Los Angeles Times*, 4 April 2001.
130. Grann, "Where W. Got Compassion."

INDEX

African Americans, 9, 29, 49, 54, 58–59, 91–93, 107, 109; and public assistance, 80–81, 121–122; social and economic conditions of, 62–64, 69–70, 72, 76; and Unigov, 104; and War on Poverty, 9, 62–90 passim

Aid to Families with Dependent Children (AFDC), 2, 6, 10, 18, 19, 23, 24, 29, 32, 33, 58–59, 111, 114–116; abolition of, 3, 10, 121, 144; attacks on, 78–81, 121–122; congregations' support of, 106; racialization of, 80–81, 121–122

American Federation of Labor-Congress of Industrial Organization (AFL-CIO), 66, 70

American Legion, 3
AmericaWorks, 143
AmeriCorps, 125
Ashcroft, John, 124
Association of Christian Churches, 114

Baptist Alliance Commission, 85
Baptist Joint Committee, 125
Baptist Ministers' Alliance, 84, 87
Barker, Paul G., 71–72
Barton, John, 6, 64–67, 69–70, 73–74, 84–86
Bayh, Birch, 86
Beechwood Garden, 115
Berger, Peter, 38
Blackburne, Cleo, 82
Boy Scouts of America, 36
Broadway Christian Center, 101, 114
Brown, Andrew J., 69–72, 87–88
Brown, Dorothy M., 7, 24
Bryan, William, 103
Burns, Jeffrey, 45
Bush, George W., 4–5, 7, 10–11, 126–127, 130, 132, 137, 144–145; and compassionate conservatism, 119, 146; and ideas about faith, 136 and support of faith-based organizations, 120, 125, 140
Butler, John, 25

Cathedral House, 99, 101. *See also* Christ Episcopal Church

Catholic Charities of Indianapolis, 7–10, 12–31 passim, 32–34, 40, 42, 46, 55, 57,144; and African Americans, 114; and counseling, 42–43, 45; and ideas about social welfare and Catholic principles, 20–26; and middle-class clientele, 50; and the Parish Outreach Program, 113; and notions of citizenship, 13, 66; and receipt of public monies, 13, 26, 27, 28, 30, 37, 112–114, 116–117, 125, 147; and War on Poverty, 113. *See also* Catholic Social Services of Indianapolis

Catholic Charities, USA, 7, 131
Catholic Community Center, 14
Catholic Conference on Industrial Problems, 19
Catholic Family Life Movement, 38
Catholic Social Services of Indianapolis, 81. *See also* Catholic Charities of Indianapolis
Catholic Youth Organization, 36
Center for Public Justice, 137
Center Township Trustees, 15–16, 19, 28, 29 30, 68, 81, 97, 113
Chao, Elaine, 136
Charitable Choice, 3–4, 10, 136–137, 140; constitutionality of, 125–126; definition of, 3, 124–125. *See also* Personal Responsibility and Work Opportunity Act
Charity, Aid, Recovery, and Empowerment Act, 120
Children's Bureau, 17, 37
Christ Episcopal Church, 98, 101, 103
Christian Inner City Association (CICA), 67–68, 74, 81, 89, 106; and housing, 109, 111; and ideas about citizenship, 67–68
Church Federation of Greater Indianapolis, 39, 40–41, 86; and adoption, 56; and housing, 108, 110–112; and urban ministry, 96–97, 108–110
citizenship and social welfare, 2, 3, 7, 89–90, 117, 123–124, 128, 146–148
Clapsaddle, Gerald, 92
Clark, William, 77, 84, 85, 107
Clinton, Bill, 120, 122, 125

169

Community Action Against Poverty (CAAP), 9, 61–90 passim, 97, 114; and the Parish Outreach Program, 113
Community Action Program, 2, 69, 75
Corporation for National and Community Service, 127

Daley, Richard, 67
Dannin, Ellen, 124
Davis, Benjamin, 86
Deer, Lewis, 101
Dewey, John, 124
Dortch, Carl, 66, 82

Economic Opportunity Act, 73
Edna Martin Center, 76
Elford, George, 107
Episcopal Community Services, 99, 118
Evangelical Christians, 57–58
Evangelical United Brethren Church, 97

FaithWorks, 10, 135, 137–139
Family Life Bureau, 38
Family Life Clinic, 40–41
Family Service Association, 8, 32, 39, 41–43, 47, 51; and adoption, 32; and counseling, 32, 42, 45, 32; and fee charges, 43; and middle-class clientele, 32–33, 39, 50; and unwed motherhood, 32, 55; and visiting homemaking, 32, 45–46
Family Week, 35
Family Welfare Society, 19, 53
Fannie Mae, 129
Farnsley, Art, 139–140
Federal Emergency Relief Act, 16
Federal highway construction, 6
Federal Housing Authority, 110, 112, 115–116
First Amendment, 4, 125
First Presbyterian Church, 105
Flanner House, 48, 82
Fletcher Place Community Center, 48, 57, 67, 99–101, 118
Fordice, Kirk, 129
Front Porch Alliance, 1, 10, 120, 134–135, 140
Fussenegger, August, 17, 18–19, 21–23, 25, 26, 27, 55

Garcia, Linda, 143
Gibson, Charles, 103
Gingrich, Newt, 145
Goldsmith, Stephen, 1, 2, 7, 10–11; and faith-based organizations, 119, 126–127, 131, 133, 140; and ideas about citizenship, 127–128; and opposition to government-run programs, 129–130, 133; and privatization, 119, 123–124, 127, 132–134; and work first strategy, 143
Gore, Al, 146
Graham, Henry, 50
Great Depression, 12, 15–16, 28, 30, 33
Great Society, 2
Green, Clifford J., 118
Gustafson, Howard, E., 66

Harrington, Michael, 9
Head Start, 61, 65–66, 69, 75–76
Henderson, Ruth, 55
Hermann, Ross, 81–82
Holy Trinity, 113
Homes Before Highways Inc., 85, 109
Hometown I, 110–111, 115. *See also* Housing Opportunities Multiplied Ecumenically
Hoosier independence, 6, 64–65, 72
Hosie, Laurence, 97
Housing Opportunities Multiplied Ecumenically (HOME), 110–112, 114–117
Hudson Institute, 126
Hulse, Lamont, 139–140

Immanuel Church, 114–115
Immanuel Counseling Center, 114–115
Indiana Girls' School, 55
Indiana University–Purdue University Indianapolis, 108
Indiana Welfare Investigation Committee, 79
Indianapolis: and anti-government sentiment, 6, 9, 16, 65, 79, 81–84, 94, 108; demographics of, 4–6, 14, 94; population of, 4; relationship to nation, 5; and white flight, 10, 91–92
Indianapolis Baptist Foresight Alliance, 85
Indianapolis Chamber of Commerce, 67, 82, 87
Indianapolis Community Fund, 33, 36
Indianapolis Community Service Council, 93, 95, 101, 104
Indianapolis Conference of Social Work, 20
Indianapolis Council of Social Agencies, 15, 17, 20
Indianapolis Housing Authority, 109
Indianapolis Neighborhood Resource Center, 139
Indianapolis Pastoral Care and Counseling Service, 43

Index

Indianapolis Redevelopment Commission, 108
Indianapolis School Board, 66
Indianapolis Social Action Council, 70
Interfaith Housing, 112
Interreligious Committee Against Poverty, 72–73, 85

Jacobs, Andrew, Jr., 86
Jewish Community Center, 36
Jewish Family Service Society, 1
Jewish Federation of Metropolitan Chicago, 131
Jewish Social Services, 39, 42, 46
Jewish Welfare Federation, 8, 50
Johnson, Lyndon B., 73, 75
Joint Urban Program, 98

Katz, Michael, 3
Kelley, Weltha, 12
Kennedy, Sheila Suess, 144
King, Martin Luther, Jr., 107
Koenig, Robert, 97
Kohls, James, 106
Krammer, Fred, 131
Ku Klux Klan, 14

Legal Services Organization, 62, 65, 75, 82, 97
Lenkowsky, Leslie, 145
Lenroot, Katharine, 17, 25
Leroy, Marian, 42
Liell, John T., 87
Lilly, Eli, 98
Lilly Endowment, 112
Lipsky, Michael, 117
Little Flower, 113
Lockerbie Street Nursery, 48
Lockfield Public Housing Project, 109
Lugar, Richard, 66, 88–89, 104
Lutheran Child Welfare, 54–55
Lutheran Family Social Services, 125
Lutheran Social Services, 131

McCalumet, Helen, 85, 87
McGowan, Raymond, 18
McKeown, Elizabeth, 7, 24
Manpower, 61, 62, 65–66
Marion County Child Guidance Clinic, 51
Marion County Department of Public Welfare, 7–8, 25–30, 64, 68, 77–78, 80, 82; and unwed motherhood, 58–60
Martindale, 61–62

Martindale Area Citizen's Service, 61, 76–77, 81–82, 88
Martinez, Mel, 136
Marydale Home, 27, 30
Maximum feasible participation of the poor, 7, 62, 64, 66–67, 70, 72, 81
Maximus, Inc., 142–143
May, Elaine Tyler, 33, 38
Mayer Chapel, 57, 101
Mayer House, 114
Medicaid, 2, 129, 142
Medicare, 2, 129
Meech, Frank, 66, 73
Melita, Rick, 143
Meridian Heights, 105
Meridian Street Methodist Church, 110
Merton, Ruben, 58
Metro Church, 99, 101
Metropolitan Center, 105
Moody Bible Institute, 69
Mothers' Pensions, 16–17
Mt. Zion Church, 110
Myers-Shirk, Susan, 35

National Catholic Community Service, 35
National Conference of Catholic Bishops, 122
National Conference of Catholic Charities, 18, 23, 25
National Council of Churches, 97, 122
National Jewish Welfare Board, 35
National Youth Administration, 23
National Youth Corps, 65–66, 69
National Youth Organization, 26
Neighborhood centers, 75, 77–78, 82, 84–85, 88
Neighborhood Community Services Program, 113
Nester, Henry G., 77
Network, 141
New Deal, 1–3, 7–8, 10, 16–19, 23–24, 28, 30, 32–33, 37, 144, 146; and Federal Emergency Relief Act, 16–17; rejection of, 121
Newton, Miller, 67, 70, 72–74, 99–100, 104
Nisbeck, John L., 80, 81, 82–83
Nixon, Richard, 88
No Child Left Behind, 137
Northeast Side Community Organization (NESCO), 107
Northwest Community Organization (NWCO), 107

O'Bannon, Frank, 10, 135
Office of Civilian Defense, 35

Office of Economic Opportunity, 62, 64, 78, 85–87
Office of Faith-Based and Community Initiatives, 125, 130
Olasky, Marvin, 145
Old Age Assistance, 23, 32
Ombudsman Act, 117
open housing bill, 63–64, 109
Operation Discovery, 69
Operation Prove It, 106
Operation Star, 69
Outpost, 100. *See also* Fletcher Place Community Center

Paige, Rod, 135
Parish Outreach Program, 113, 117. *See also* Catholic Charities of Indianapolis
Payne, James, 126, 131, 133
Personal Responsibility and Work Opportunity Act, 3, 10, 120–122, 124, 140
Powell, Adam Clayton, 71
Presbyterian Church U.S.A., 96
Privatization, 1, 10, 120, 122–123, 127, 144

Quadragesimo anno (1931), 18

Raines, Franklin D., 129
Rerum novarum, 18
Riley-Lockerbie Ministerial Association, 106
Ritter, Joseph E., 12, 18
Rivers, Eugene, 134
Rodgers, Melissa, 125
Roosevelt, Franklin D., 18, 121
Ryan, John, 18–19

St. Andrew's Catholic Church, 113
St. Elizabeth's Home, 1, 53–54, 56
St. John Baptist Church, 69
Saint Louis University, 12, 21
St. Rita's Catholic Church, 61, 76
St. Vincent de Paul Society, 144
Salvation Army, 10, 35, 100–101, 117, 131
Sanders, Mozell, 84, 87, 107
Sawyer, George, 83
Schmidlin, Donald, 88, 113
Second Vatican Council, 114
Sells, Ray, 107
Shack, 100–101. *See also* Salvation Army
Sherman, Amy, 126
Sisters of the Good Shepherd, 27
Skocpol, Theda, 3
Smith, David, 66, 70

Smith, Robert, 107
Smith, Stephen Rathgeb, 117
Social Security Act, 2, 6, 18, 23; 1967 amendments to, 3, 109
Solinger, Rickie, 53
Southern Christian Leadership Conference (SCLC), 70–71, 107
Stanton, William, 64, 77–78, 80–81
Strange, Bernard, 76
Stroh, Byron, 102
Suemma Coleman Home, 1, 53–56
Swift, Linton B., 33

Teen Challenge, 145–146
Temporary Assistance to Needy Families (TANF), 121–122, 138, 140–141
Ten Point Coalition, 134
Texas Commission on Alcohol and Drug Abuse, 145
Third Christian Church, 105
Thurston, Anthony, 102
Title IV-A, 109–110
Title X, 114
Title XX, 117

Unigov, 104
Union of American Hebrew Congregations, 122
United Church Missionary Society, 114
United Methodist Church, 96
United Service Organization (USO), 35
United Southeast Community Organization (USCO), 106–107
United Southside Community Organization (USSCO), 107
United States Department of Education, 135; and novice applicant rule, 136
United States Department of Health and Human Services (HHS), 135; and Compassion Fund, 135
United States Department of Housing and Urban Development (HUD), 135–136
United States Department of Labor, 135–136
Unwed motherhood, 52–56, 58, 60, 78–80. *See also* Catholic Charities of Indianapolis; Church Federation of Greater Indianapolis; Suemma Coleman Home; St. Elizabeth's Home
Urban ministry, 9, 91–118 passim; disillusionment with, 115–117
Urban Mission Council of Indianapolis, 102

Index

Urban Task Force, 108. *See also* Church Federation of Greater Indianapolis

VanBeten, John, 66

Walkowitz, Daniel, 20
Walls, John W., 88
War on Poverty, 2, 7, 9, 61–90 passim, 93, 94, 96, 129, 132, 147; and Catholics, 68–69, 76; in Chicago, 67, 113; in Mississippi, 69; in Philadelphia, 69; and Protestant congregations, 105
Weber, Bruce L., 66

Welfare Rights Organization, 78, 81, 99, 101, 114
Wellstone, Paul, 141
Wheeler Mission, 28, 58
White House Conference on Family Life, 37
Williams, Faye, 61, 76–78, 82, 113
Williams, Susan, 140
Works Progress Administration (WPA), 7, 22, 23, 28–29
World War II, 32, 35, 63

YMCA, 35, 36

Mary L. Mapes is a U.S. social historian specializing in the relationship between public and private social welfare agencies. After receiving her Ph.D. from Michigan State University in 1998, she worked as a research associate at the Polis Center at IUPUI. She is currently Adjunct Professor of History at Lake Forest College, where she teaches American history.

UNIVERSITY OF ST. THOMAS LIBRARIES

HV 99 .I5 M37 2004
Mapes, Mary L.
A public charity

WITHDRAWN
UST
Libraries